THE CR
MOTHE

There are a few significant books on my bookshelf about the
important issue of spiritual fathering and mothering, but none of
them tops this one. Larry Kreider has reached into the storehouse
of his unique experience and insight to offer us what will no
doubt become a new standard on the subject. Because Larry's
understanding of the role of spiritual parents in the family of God
is so profound, I enthusiastically recommend this book to you.

Dr. David Cannistraci
Senior Pastor, GateWay City Church, San Jose, California
Author, *God's Vision for Your Church*

Larry Kreider is a true servant to the Church, a leader whose
dimension of effectiveness in advancing the Kingdom and shaping
leaders evidences a level of gifting and humility that is so apostolic
that it doesn't need that title to certify it. I trust this man because
his heart is pure and his mind is clear.

Jack W. Hayford
Founder and Chancellor, The King's University, Los Angeles and Dallas

Larry Kreider's book *The Cry for Spiritual Mothers and Fathers*
reflects the values and vision he has imparted to DOVE Christian
Fellowship International. The wisdom of these pages shows why
DOVE has produced a stable, growing apostolic stream. When
many American movements have declined or disappeared, Larry
shows the way to growth and stability through spiritual parenting.

Dr. Daniel C. Juster
Director, Tikkun International

I devoured Larry's book in one reading. Now I want to go back
and digest it so I can pass on to others what I have learned.

Floyd McClung
Founder, All Nations, Cape Town, South Africa

Once again Larry Kreider has pioneered the way for others with this new book. He combines experience, knowledge and passion to guide us into Kingdom community. Read it with a highlighter in your hand and a person you wish to mentor in your heart!

Ralph Neighbour
Touch Ministries, Texas

Larry has done it again! He's put cutting-edge concepts into laymen's language. This is by far the best book on spiritual parenting that I have read on this subject. The combination of biblical principles and practical examples easily goes cross-cultural. This should be read by senior church and missions' leaders, but also by young leaders who can begin to apply the teachings immediately. Larry has true authority and experience that many will learn from. Buy numerous copies of this book, practice the principles and, whatever your ministry is, it will be multiplied into many future generations. Give this book away to faithful men and women now.

Jim Orred
Youth With A Mission, Kailua-Kona, Hawaii

Larry Kreider is a spiritual father! In his book *The Cry for Spiritual Mothers and Fathers*, he not only extends a call to those who have a heart to train and establish others, but shares practical wisdom that helps one generation establish the next. This book provides how-to blueprints and challenges all of us need to move beyond our dysfunctional and abusive relationships of the past to become models of relationship building for a new generation. *The Cry for Spiritual Mothers and Fathers* will help you to develop a new lifestyle—after all, we are always influencing someone.

Dr. Chuck D. Pierce
President, Glory of Zion International Ministries
President, Global Spheres, Inc.

Larry Kreider has identified the key issue in the Church world today: Will the Church become a parenting force to impart health to a broken world? The implications of the spirit of fathering affect every area of personal and corporate spiritual life. There is an urgent call today for relationships that provide healthy spiritual nurture and authority. God is calling us to actively give ourselves to both being spiritually fathered as well as becoming spiritual fathers. Larry Kreider not only teaches on spiritual fathering, he *is* a spiritual father—and through his words, the Lord calls us to maturity.

Dr. Robert Stearns
Founder and Executive Director, Eagles' Wings

The Cry for Spiritual Mothers and Fathers is much more than a road map showing how we who are mature Christians must nurture the newer generations. It is all of that, but it is also an awesome word for cutting-edge leadership in today's Church. I, for one, want to be the kind of fatherly leader that Larry Kreider urges us to be.

C. Peter Wagner
Vice President, Global Spheres, Inc.

What a great book! It's down to earth, practical, understandable and applicable to mentoring emerging leaders today—it's authentic. Larry Kreider is a father in the Church today. He writes out of who he is and the practical experience he has gained over the years. This book is a must for those who are mentoring or discipling others.

Barbara J. Yoder
Senior Pastor, Shekinah International Apostolic Center, Ann Arbor, Michigan

THE CRY FOR SPIRITUAL MOTHERS & FATHERS

The Next Generation
Needs You to Be a
Spiritual Mentor

LARRY KREIDER

Author of *The 3 Loves* and *Starting a House Church*

Regal

For more information and
special offers from Regal Books, email us at
subscribe@regalbooks.com

Published by Regal
From Gospel Light
Ventura, California, U.S.A.
www.regalbooks.com
Printed in the U.S.A.

Library of Congress Cataloging-in-Publication Data
Kreider, Larry.
The cry for spiritual mothers and fathers: the next generation needs
you to be a spiritual mentor / Larry Kreider.
pages cm
Includes bibliographical references.
ISBN 978-0-8307-6874-5 (trade paper)
1. Spiritual direction. I. Title.
BV4408.5.K74 2014
253.5'3—dc23
2013031690

Rights for publishing this book in other languages are contracted by Gospel Light
Worldwide, the international nonprofit ministry of Gospel Light. Gospel Light Worldwide
also provides publishing and technical assistance to international publishers dedicated to
producing Sunday School and Vacation Bible School curricula and books in the languages
of the world. For additional information, visit www.gospellightworldwide.org;
write to Gospel Light Worldwide, P.O. Box 3875, Ventura, CA 93006;
or send an e-mail to info@gospellightworldwide.org.

To my wife, LaVerne,
to my family
and to everyone who reads this book and
becomes a spiritual mother or father.
May you find great joy in fulfilling your call from God.

CONTENTS

Part III: Practical Insights for Spiritual Mothers and Fathers

ACKNOWLEDGMENTS

A special thanks goes to Karen Ruiz and Lou Ann Good, who do superb jobs as my writing assistant, and editor, respectively.

Thank you to those who gave valuable insight to this book: Sarah Sauder, Peter Bunton, Steve Prokopchak and Ron Myer.

And thanks to the entire Regal team. It is a joy to work with you!

FOREWORD

I have waited a long time for this book. There is not another one like it anywhere. *The Cry for Spiritual Mothers and Fathers* blends sound teaching on how to develop each member of the church for ministry, with spiritual fathering and mothering at every level of the Church, all the while honoring the role of the senior pastor. Larry Kreider does this in the context of "every member" ministry in small groups. What pastor wouldn't want every member of his or her church engaged in using his or her spiritual gifts for effective ministry? Because *The Cry for Spiritual Mothers and Fathers* addresses such an important subject, it should be required reading for the staff and small-group leaders of every local church.

The Cry for Spiritual Mothers and Fathers addresses many of the leadership issues pastors face in discipling church members and raising up emerging leaders, and it does so from a firm foundation of biblical truth. What we don't need is another book on spiritual leadership filled with anecdotes but void of scriptural principle. This book avoids that temptation. Larry combines encouraging, down-to-earth, helpful illustrations in every chapter, and he does this with plenty of scriptural references. This book allows us to know what Larry believes and why he believes it.

Larry reminds us that churches are only as effective as the relational ties the church members have with each other. And then he goes on to demonstrate how to build that kind of church. "Becoming a Spiritual Family" will set the standard for leadership in your church or ministry. By taking staff members and small-group leaders through an in-depth study of this book, a leader will save him- or herself many heartaches. It helps build a common framework for what people can expect from their leaders, what leaders should expect from one another, and how to raise up father-leaders. This book will help define how leadership works and what to do when leaders fail in a church or ministry.

While affirming the need for spiritual fathers and mothers, Larry avoids the excesses of spiritual control and from top-down church life. He believes—and demonstrates repeatedly—that when the believer-priests are mobilized to use their gifts, a struggling local church is transformed into a New Testament local church.

As a pastor with a vision for those leaders I train to be involved in effective, small-group ministry, I want my trainees to catch Larry Kreider's vision for spiritual fathering and mothering. As Larry has so effectively communicated in this book, spiritual parenting is something every person can do. When the saints believe this and when we as leaders are focused with single-minded determination to see it become a reality, it will happen. Then God will have a people for Himself that reflects His glory.

A book that helps us know how to go about raising up spiritual fathers and mothers, while warning us of the pitfalls and dangers along the way, is invaluable. I devoured Larry's book in one reading, and now I want to go back and digest it, so I can pass on to others what I have learned. I hope you will do the same.

Floyd McClung
Founder, All Nations
Cape Town, South Africa

A NOTE FROM THE AUTHOR

I am excited about the release of this book. My wife, LaVerne, and I have more than 40 years experience serving as spiritual parents to spiritual sons and daughters scattered around the world. As we have attempted to follow Jesus and His model of making disciples, we have learned—through the help of the Holy Spirit and through the school of experience—so much about this incredible privilege.

In the year 2000, I wrote my first book on this subject, *The Cry for Spiritual Fathers and Mothers: Compelling Vision for Authentic, Nurturing Relationships Within Today's Church.* Eight years later, Regal Books asked me to consider writing on the subject of spiritual mentoring. In response, I took much of what I had written about spiritual fathering and mothering in my first book and added more of what I had learned in the intervening years about spiritual mentoring. The book *Authentic Spiritual Mentoring: Nurturing Young Believers Toward Spiritual Maturity* was released in 2008.

Through conversations I had with my friends at Gospel Light during the past year, it became clear that I should combine/revise what I had written in the previous two books and add important practical truths and the lessons I have been learning about being an effective spiritual parent—all in order to help others know how to empower the next generation. The result is the book you hold in your hands: *The Cry for Spiritual Mothers and Fathers: The Next Generation Needs You to Be a Spiritual Mentor.*

Jesus became a spiritual parent to His disciples, and Paul the apostle told the believers in the early church:

> We were gentle among you, like a mother caring for her little children. We loved you so much that we were delighted to share with you not only the gospel of God but our lives as well, because you had become so dear to us.
>
> For you know that we dealt with each of you as a father deals with his own children, encouraging, comforting and urging you to live lives worthy of God, who calls you into his kingdom and glory.
>
> For what is our hope, our joy, or the crown in which we will glory in the presence of our Lord Jesus when he comes? Is it not you? Indeed, you are our glory and joy (1 Thess. 2:7-8,11-12,19-20).

Jesus and Paul set the example for us by becoming spiritual parents to the next generation, and they call us to follow in their steps.

As you apply the biblical truths presented in this book and follow the pattern modeled by Jesus Christ 2,000 years ago, the Lord will use you to change our world.

Of particular importance to this book is the addition of questions meant to enhance studying the book in a small-group setting or in your personal study. Located at the end of each chapter, the questions are intended to help you apply what you have read and allow you to develop into the spiritual mother or father God has destined you to become.

May the Lord bless you abundantly as you fulfill His destiny for your life and as you experience the joy and the blessing of becoming a spiritual father or mother.

Larry Kreider

Part I

UNDERSTANDING THE IMPORTANCE OF SPIRITUAL MOTHERING AND FATHERING

1

Calling All Believers

Key: Everyone is called to be a spiritual mother or father.

Recently I spoke to a group of young people at one of America's dynamic megachurches, and a young man approached me after the session. "I'm on staff here, but I'm leaving next month," he confided.

I was puzzled. "Why?"

He looked deeply into my eyes and said, "Larry, if just one person in leadership in this church sat down with me for an hour once a month for a cup of coffee and asked me how I was doing, I would stay." The young man was looking for a spiritual father—someone to spend some time with him, someone who could offer support and guidance and feedback as he learned to use his gifts and talents within the church. But everyone was too busy: More attention was paid to the church's many programs than to individual people.

A few years ago, I was traveling with a well-known evangelist in New Zealand; and in a tired, almost wistful voice he said something to me that I will never forget: "Larry, you know what I really need? I need a father." Here was a powerfully anointed leader, highly successful as an evangelist, whose greatest need was for someone who cared deeply enough to interact with him. He needed someone to act as a sounding board and to help him turn problems into opportunities. He was longing for a spiritual father—a seasoned Christian man to encourage him and give him advice and support.

Another time, LaVerne and I were visited by a new Christian who was depressed and discouraged. "LaVerne and Larry," she said to my wife and me, "I know the Lord has changed my life, but there is so much I don't understand. I'm not sure if I'll make it. I just can't decipher half of what I hear in church." Then she admitted the true cry of her heart: "I really need someone to help me understand the things I'm taught. I need someone to help me grow up spiritually."

An elderly pastor I once knew was ready to retire and hand over the baton to the younger leadership, but he had not trained anyone to take his place. He nearly wept as he admitted that he had somehow missed the mark when it came to training and nurturing his spiritual sons. They did not honor him or look to him as a father.

I hear stories like these again and again. As I travel throughout the world, training leaders and potential leaders week after week, I see a consistent and desperate need for believers who are willing to serve as spiritual fathers and mothers. Whether the Christians are new to the faith, have been practicing the faith for many years or even are pastors, the need is still the same: Deep down inside, there is a longing to be mothered or fathered. God has created us with a need to feel connected in relationships, but a painful lack of nurturing, support and interaction in the Church has created a void.

More and more believers are awakening to the need. A few years ago in our county in Pennsylvania, there was a powerful move of God among young people. It started when a few youth got serious about reaching their peers for Christ. The Bible study they started with a handful of kids grew to more than 1,000 young people coming together every Tuesday night. One of the young leaders told me why he felt the Lord chose our area for a move of God: "We had spiritual fathers here who were ready and willing to serve and encourage us."

Because spiritual fathers and mothers poured into these young people what the Lord had given them—because they had mentored the young men and women—young leaders were produced who were prepared to become spiritual parents themselves. The next generation felt that they were loved and trained well enough to pass on a lasting legacy of their own.

> The Uncommon Individual Foundation, an organization devoted to mentoring research and training, . . . reports that mentoring is the third most powerful relationship for influencing human behavior, after marriage and the extended family.
>
> Randy MacFarland, who helps train mentors as Vice President of Training and Mentoring at Denver Seminary, says, "When we consider the fragmentation of the family, the speed of change demanding the constant learning of new skills, and our mobile society separating extended family members, the need for mentoring increases. . . . We often forget how powerful it is when someone believes in us."[1]

That's what spiritual mentors, or spiritual parents, do: They believe in the younger generation. They help shape lives while passing on a legacy.

But what happens when a generation is left to its own resources and is not provided with mentoring, or parenting, care?

One Way to Preserve Life

A few years ago I visited Pilanesberg Park, a South African game preserve, and learned that not too many years earlier, the survival of the white rhinoceros in this game park was in question. Several of these endangered rhinos had been found slaughtered. The game wardens decided to electronically tag and track the remaining rhinos, placing video cameras in strategic locations to record any evidence of foul play.

After tracking the rhinos and reviewing the video footage, park officials were astounded to discover that young bull elephants were harassing the rhinos without provocation. Although the behavior was unnatural for them, these teenaged elephants were chasing the white rhinos for long distances, throwing sticks at them until they were exhausted and then stomping them to death. Why were these young elephants acting so violently? The answer was found in a decision made 20 years earlier.

At that time, park officials decided to transport some elephants from another national park into the Pilanesberg preserve, because the other location was unable to support the increasing elephant population. The elephants too large to transport were killed, including a number of mature bulls. Only younger elephants were sent to Pilanesberg, where they matured without the presence and influence of mature males. By investigating the rhinos' mysterious deaths, park rangers and scientists discovered that without the presence of mature bulls, the young male elephants were suffering from excessive aggression and becoming violent.

To remedy the situation and preserve the white rhino population, park officials killed five of the most aggressive young bull elephants and then imported older bulls in order to provide an influence for the remaining young males. The older bulls began to assume their place among the herd as fathers and disciplinarians, and the young bulls learned quickly that they were no match for the more mature elephants.

Some park officials were surprised when it became apparent that the young bulls actually enjoyed their relationship with the older, more mature males. The former lawbreakers returned to normal patterns of elephant behavior, and after the arrival of the mature elephants, there were no more reports of dead rhinos.

The Need to Equip the Young for Growth

The elephant story illustrates what younger Christians can gain if they have spiritual mentors to help them by supporting, counseling and teaching them. Of course, the story also demonstrates what happens when seasoned Christians fail to act as spiritual parents. When mature Christians neglect to assume their responsibility to share their wisdom and love with younger Christians, the younger ones are not fully equipped for the task that lies ahead. They may be energetic and gifted, but without direction and loving oversight, they have a tendency to get off track—or even to trample those in their path.

There is a desperate need for spiritually mature men and women to mentor younger Christians, helping them to clarify what really matters in life and work. Spiritual parents who act as mature coaches can help younger believers achieve their dreams and visions and feel connected as they integrate life and work and grow to maturity.

Instead of developing deep and nurturing relationships with spiritual parents, today's believers are encouraged to participate in church services, Bible studies, para-church organizations or evangelistic ministries in order to bolster his or her faith and "grow strong in the Lord." The theory is that more teaching from God's Word plus more ministry participation equals more spiritual maturity. As important as these involvements may be, such a faulty supposition leads to believers inhaling message after message, book after book, CD after CD, seminar after seminar—all in order to fill a void for real relationships.

The results are Christians who become fat spiritually and fail to interpret what they are learning so that they can pass it on to others. These Christians do not know how to meaningfully and sacrificially impart their lives to others because they have never been properly parented. Without role models, they remain spiritual infants, needing to be spoon-fed by the pastor or some other Christian worker.

But as God's people, believers need to grow up and out of the spoon-fed stage. This growth is very difficult to do alone, just as natural infants cannot thrive if left on their own. Babies need the care and nurture of parents, just as believers need practical input from loving spiritual parents who delight when their children reach their full potential in Christ.

Countless examples of spiritual parenting appear in the Scriptures. Jesus modeled spiritual fatherhood to the 12 disciples. Paul discipled young Timothy. Elizabeth became a spiritual mother to Mary, the mother of Jesus. Elijah became a spiritual parent to Elisha. Moses trained Joshua to take his place to lead the children of Israel into the Promised Land. In many of these examples, the one being guided was nurtured and prepared to stand in the place of his mentor to eventually fulfill God's greater purpose. In the case of Elijah and Elisha, the spiritual son even received an impartation of double anointing from his spiritual father (see 2 Kings 2:9-10). Throughout Scripture, we read about these one-on-one spiritual parenting relationships and how they produce a rich legacy of impartation to future generations. We need this kind of connection and impartation today.

In the book *Connecting: The Mentoring Relationships You Need to Succeed in Life,* the authors begin their book with a surprising statement: "Research on biblical leaders led to a startling conclusion—few leaders finish well."[2] They go on to say that in cases when leaders in the Bible did finish well, "their relationship to another person significantly enhanced their development."[3]

The apostle Paul knew that imparting a spiritual legacy should be his highest aim, and he was determined to finish well with strong relationships. He was a role model and spiritual father to many in the Early Church. He very clearly spelled out spiritual fathering as his leadership model: "Follow my example, as I follow the example of Christ" (1 Cor. 11:1); "whatever you have learned or received or heard from me, or seen in me—put it into practice" (Phil. 4:9). In other words, "Let me be a spiritual father to you. Let me be your role model. Then go and do the same."

After a long absence from his spiritual children in the church at Thessalonica, Paul wrote a letter to them out of his concern that they might interpret his physical absence as proof he didn't care about them. He ended his letter by praying, not only that God would direct his way back to them, but also that they would love others in the same way that he had loved them (see 1 Thess. 3:11-12). He expected them to take up the loving responsibility of being spiritual parents for others. The New Testament Church was to model a growing and developing family. Every Christian was to become a spiritual father or spiritual mother!

The Call to All Believers

Apparently the church at Corinth needed some extra encouragement from Paul to take up the loving responsibility of becoming spiritual parents. Paul challenged the Corinthian church not to overlook this need: "For though you might have ten thousand instructors in Christ, yet you do not have many fathers" (1 Cor. 4:15, *NKJV*). The Corinthian church had many teachers in their spiritual lives but few spiritual mothers or fathers. Since the time Paul had brought the Corinthians to faith in Christ, many instructors had taught God's Word to them. They had heard these teachers and faithfully attended church services, but they then had become arrogant in their knowledge of the gospel (see 1 Cor. 4:18). They were proud of what they knew, but they were immature as believers. They lacked true spiritual parents, or spiritual mentors, to give them proper training and nurturing, to help them put their knowledge into life practice.

Paul knew that in order for the Corinthian church to grow spiritually, all of the believers had to be in vital relationships with others who had gone down the same spiritual road before; otherwise, the believers would be content to do what the instructors told them to do rather than learning how to hear from God themselves. This was wisdom that could only be learned as they received mentoring from a loving spiritual father. To jumpstart the process, Paul told the Corinthians that he was sending Timothy to "remind you of my way of life in Christ Jesus" (1 Cor. 4:17). Paul had trained Timothy, his beloved and trustworthy spiritual son, and now Timothy would come to train them. Paul trusted Timothy to help the wayward Corinthian church because Paul had trained him like a son. Timothy was ready to impart *his* spiritual fatherhood to the Corinthian church. With Paul and Timothy's example, the Corinthian church would soon be producing their own spiritual sons and daughters. Paul was confident that when believers saw spiritual mothering and fathering modeled, they would be equipped to pass on that legacy to the next generation.

It was a lack of mature leadership in the Corinthian church that stunted the believers' spiritual growth. Unequipped to grow up spiritually, they struggled to find their identity in Christ. They did not know who they were in the Lord. Deficient of true spiritual mothers and fathers to model parenthood, the Corinthian church had become a system that produced programs and teachers, not a family producing sons and daughters.

Because they did not have their identity grounded in Christ, the Corinthians sought it through their favorite leader: "I follow Paul,...I follow Apollos" (1 Cor. 3:4). Paul chided the Corinthian church for its lack of maturity, making it plain that while people have roles to play, only God is clearly the source of any good thing, and they should ultimately follow only Him. What they really needed were spiritual mothers and fathers to pay close attention to them so that they could be nudged toward maturity. They needed spiritual parents to sow into their lives, who expected them eventually to become spiritual parents themselves, creating a spiritual harvest of believers with Christ-grounded identities who would continue to multiply down through the generations.

God's intention is to produce spiritual parents who are willing to nurture spiritual children and help them grow into spiritual parents. This is a fulfillment of the Lord's promise to "turn the hearts of the fathers to the children, and the hearts of the children to their fathers" (Mal. 4:6). The Lord is restoring harmony between mothers and fathers—both natural and spiritual—and their children, so that parents can freely impart their inheritance to the next generation. Children need parents who nurture strong character and assure them that they are valuable—that they are gifts from God. As such children mature, they in turn must nurture the next generation.

Everyone is called to be a spiritual mother or spiritual father: Each of us is nurtured as a child to become a parent.

Key Questions for Practical Application

1. Who needs spiritual mothers and fathers, and why?
2. Who are some real-life models of spiritual parenting that you have seen?
3. When and how should the groundwork to become spiritual parents be laid?

2

Making a Spiritual Investment

Key: Spiritual children are our inheritance.

Wouldn't it be great if someone saw your potential in Christ and decided to invest in your life? What do you think would happen if more Christians made themselves available in spiritual parenting relationships?

My friend Don Finto, who for many years served as the senior pastor of Belmont Church in Nashville, Tennessee, has a great passion to father younger men in ministry. One of his more famous spiritual sons, the singer and musician Michael W. Smith, says the effect of Don's mentoring of him has been profound:

> I don't think I'd be where I am today if it hadn't been for Don. I've saved all his letters. He has encouraged me in so many ways—my self-confidence and who I am in the Lord—pulling stuff out of me that nobody ever was able to pull out.[1]

The potential for relationships such as Don and Michael's in today's Church is truly enormous. Geese fly in a V formation, because the aerodynamics of the V enable the geese to fly over 70 percent farther than if they fly alone. As each bird flaps its wings, an updraft is created for the bird behind it. When the bird in front gets tired, it moves back in the formation. Geese go a lot farther when they work together. That is the point of a spiritual parenting relationship: We can go a lot farther spiritually when we work together in family-like units to reach the world.

Leaving a Spiritual Legacy

Have you ever heard of the Shakers? They were a religious group that flourished in the early nineteenth century that built large communities in the eastern United States. Because of their peculiar practice of trembling at their meetings, they were called Shakers.

Today, there is just one active Shaker community left, and it has only a few members, so the Shakers are virtually history. The most visible trace of the group is the simple, well-made furniture they crafted. Why has this once-thriving group come so close to dying out? Because the Shakers believe in and practice celibacy above marriage. They have little opportunity to multiply. The religious revivals that once brought many converts to Shakerism lost momentum, and the group began its decline in the late 1800s.

When we do not produce children, our legacy is stunted and our posterity dies, very much as has happened with the Shakers. Without spiritual fathers and mothers to raise the next generation, we are in grave danger of dying out. All that's left will be religious furniture stuck in a corner somewhere, occasionally admired with a sense of nostalgia and regret.

For many years, my extended family—all the aunts, uncles, brothers, sisters, cousins, nephews and nieces who are connected to the Kreider family tree—gathered together for a reunion. When my grandparents were alive, I noticed how they looked at each other with a twinkle in their eyes at these family gatherings. They knew we were all there because of them, and it gave them deep satisfaction to see their posterity.

The Lord wants to see spiritual families continually reproducing in each generation down through the ages. The apostle Paul was thinking in terms of *four* generations when he called Timothy his son and exhorted him to find faithful men to whom he could impart what Paul had taught him: "And the things you [second generation] have heard me [first generation] say in the presence of many witnesses entrust to reliable men [third generation] who will also be qualified to teach others [fourth generation]" (2 Tim. 2:2). Paul was thinking about his spiritual legacy and speaking as a spiritual father to his spiritual son, who would in turn give him spiritual grandchildren and then great-grandchildren. The entire Bible was written from a family perspective. It was natural for Paul to think in terms of spiritual posterity, because that is how biblical society was set up and the way God intended it to be. The Lord has a generational perspective and we must as well.

Multiplying Our Inheritance

God has called us to become spiritual fathers and mothers in our generation. With this comes the expectation that our spiritual children will have their own spiritual children who will have even more spiritual children, thus providing ever-increasing multiplication.

Your inheritance will be all the spiritual children that you can someday present to Jesus Christ. No matter what you do—whether you are a housewife, a student, a worker in a factory, a pastor of a church, a missionary, or the head of a large corporation—you have the divine blessing and responsibility to birth spiritual children, grandchildren and great-grandchildren. You are called to impart to others the rich inheritance God has promised.

While I was serving as a pastor, I was once asked to minister at a training seminar to equip church leaders to become effective spiritual fathers and mothers. The seminar was at a four-year-old church in Lincoln, California, pastored by Daren Laws. I was amazed at what I experienced there. More than 80 percent of the people in the church were new believers. Even the mayor and his wife had come to faith in Christ and were members of the congregation. This fledgling church was already 600 people strong and focused on training spiritual fathers and mothers to minister to young Christians. Daren and his team focused, not on church programs, but on Jesus and on spiritual parenting.

At the Lincoln church, when a person came to Christ, he or she was immediately invited to a home church (or small group). There the new Christian was connected by relationships into the Body of Christ. A spiritual parent nurtured the new believer until he or she could become a spiritual parent him- or herself, and a new generation of believers was birthed! That church in California understands multiplying their inheritance.

I like how Abraham responded when the Lord showed him the stars in the heaven and promised him descendants as numerous as the stars: "And [Abraham] believed in the LORD" (Gen. 15:6). What did he believe the Lord for? His inheritance! We, too, need to "believe in the Lord" for many spiritual children. We can trust God to do it. It may not happen overnight, but it *will* happen when we trust in God's faithfulness and obey our calling to spiritual parenting.

After ministering at a church in Dallas, Texas, a young man holding a Bible ran up to me and wanted to tell his story:

> My folks are not Christians, but recently I opened up this Bible I found lying on the coffee table. After reading in it, I realized I needed Jesus. I gave my life to Christ and then drove around with my Bible in hand looking for a church family. I found a church building near where I live and walked in.
>
> The first person to greet me was a young lady, and after telling her my story, she called her father over and said, "Tell my dad what you told me."
>
> The dad listened to my testimony with interest and then examined the Bible I held in my hands. "Fifteen years ago," he said, "I witnessed to a man I served with in the military. He declined to receive the Lord but agreed to take the Bible you are holding. The man I witnessed to was your father!"

The young Texan went on to tell me the rest of the story. He was now engaged to marry the young lady he met at the church building, and they were both excited about serving as small-group leaders. The spiritual lineage begun by her father would continue. What an awesome story of spiritual posterity in God's kingdom!

Impacting Generations

The Lord wants us to be fruitful and multiply (see Gen. 1:28). Our God is a God of multiplication.

Multiplication is a fact of nature. As a farm boy, I once counted the kernels on a healthy stalk of corn and found there to be 1,200 kernels in the first generation. Consider this: If each of those kernels were planted, by the next generation there would be 1,440,000 kernels of corn! In the same way, healthy cells in the body multiply and result in growth of the body. A living cell is in a state of constant reproductive activity.

The Early Church documented in the book of Acts multiplied rapidly, because they functioned in close relationship with each other, and this healthy activity and interdependence resulted in multiplication (see Acts 2:47). They understood the value of small groups meeting in homes to aid in nurturing believers through spiritual family relationships.

As the Lord restores spiritual family life into His kingdom today, the Church will also multiply rapidly. We must be ready. We must properly train and prepare spiritual sons and daughters so that Christ may be formed in them. Romans 8:19 says, "The creation waits in eager expectation for the sons of God to be revealed." When Christ is fully formed in His people, creation is going to sit up and take notice!

Paul was longing to see his spiritual children in Thessalonica when he wrote to them: "For what is our hope, our joy, or the crown in which we will glory in the presence of our Lord Jesus when he comes? Is it not you? Indeed, you are our glory and joy" (1 Thess. 2:19-20). A few verses earlier, the apostle had just told the Thessalonian believers that he was like a spiritual mother and father to them (see 1 Thess. 2:7-11). Then he made clear that his spiritual children were his glory and joy—his inheritance! Paul rejoiced like a winner receiving a crown of victory at the games when he thought of the spiritual children and grandchildren he would present to Christ. He knew in his bones that our spiritual children and grandchildren would be not only our spiritual posterity but also part of his! And this process of spiritual multiplication is to continue on from generation to generation.

Several years ago I was in Barbados training church leaders and believers to be spiritual parents. The day I was to come back to the United States, Bill Landis, a missionary who leads Youth With A Mission's Caribbean ministry, invited me to his home before going to the airport. Bill and his family, along with a team of leaders, were in the process of equipping Bajan Christians to become spiritual leaders. On this visit to his house, Bill told me some interesting history about the tiny island nation.

He explained that years ago, many people in Barbados were brought as slaves to the island from Gambia and other West African nations. But now, Bill and his team are training Bajan Christians as missionaries so that they can return to their ancestral country of Gambia and lead Muslim Gambians to Christ. With a common heritage, it is the ideal match.

Then Bill said something that moved me deeply: "Larry, do you realize the people being reached in Gambia are a part of your spiritual heritage? You were one of my spiritual fathers, so you have a part in the ongoing legacy."

As I sat on the plane returning to the United States, I was dumbfounded at the significance of Bill's words. Years ago, long before I was a pastor or an author or a church leader, I was a young chicken farmer from Lancaster County, Pennsylvania, who led a Bible study of young people. During that time, I was a spiritual father to Bill.

Bill was a spiritual father to those Bajans he had discipled in Barbados. The Bajan Christians who were now going to Africa to lead Gambians to Christ were like my spiritual grandchildren, and the spiritual children they birthed and nurtured in Gambia would be my great-grandchildren. Generations to come would receive God's promises because a chicken farmer had been obedient to God's call to disciple a bunch of rambunctious teenagers 30 years earlier. Yes, this was part of my spiritual legacy. As I pondered this reality, I was deeply moved. I was the beneficiary of a large inheritance that had multiplied beyond my wildest dreams!

As a young man in my 20s, I had spent time with Bill, simply imparting to him Christ and His Word. Bill did the same with many others. This pattern continues to this day, and it will continue for many tomorrows. I love the way Paul the apostle saw himself as a spiritual parent intent on seeing Christ formed in those he served: "My dear children, for whom I am again in the pains of childbirth until Christ is formed in you" (Gal. 4:19). Becoming a spiritual parent is all about presenting to the Lord others mature in Christ. "We proclaim him, admonishing and teaching everyone with all wisdom, so that we may present everyone perfect in Christ" (Col. 1:28).

Reaping the Harvest

We live in exciting days in the history of the Church. I believe we are on the verge of a great end-time harvest (see Rev. 7:9). Statistics show that the ratio of people being saved today compared to 20 years ago is escalating.[2] Clearly, the wind of the Holy Spirit is sweeping our world in an unprecedented manner! In the next years as we race toward the last chapter in history, we must prepare for hundreds of thousands of people who will come into the kingdom of God in our communities.

Jesus told us to be constantly alert and ready: "Do you not say, 'Four months more and then the harvest'? I tell you, open your eyes and look at the fields! They are ripe for harvest" (John 4:35). I grew up on a farm. I know that various crops are ready to be harvested at different times of the year. We had to be alert, with our barns and equipment ready, so that we could harvest our crops at just the right time to reap a good harvest.

Down through the ages, the Lord has continually drawn people to Himself as many were harvested into His kingdom. Sometimes, however, a large portion of the harvest was lost, because Christians were not alert and ready. It seems to me that one such huge harvest for which the Church was not prepared occurred from the late 1960s to the mid-1970s. It was called the Jesus People movement. This harvest began when a number of believers in Christ entered the hippie counterculture community and shared the gospel of Jesus Christ with them, resulting in a massive number of conversions to Christianity among young people. By early 1971, there were Jesus People coffeehouses, communes and other enterprises in every state and province across the United States and Canada.

But most members of the Church were unprepared for this radical new breed of Christian. The tension between the Jesus People and established churches was a source of irritation both for the Jesus People—who saw the Church as slow moving and steeped in tradition and legalism—and for the members of the institutional Church—who often could not understand kids with long hair and sandals. Although some churches and Christian communities did welcome these new converts with open arms and did disciple them, many new believers fell by the wayside and became disillusioned, until they were eventually lost to the Body of Christ.

If the Church had been prepared and been more understanding of and compassionate toward those young people during that huge revival, I believe the harvest could have been much greater. In my opinion, there were simply not enough spiritual mentors willing to put their arms around these "Jesus freaks" and nurture them as babes in Christ until they could stand on their own. May we not make the same mistake in this generation!

The Lord is calling for thousands of spiritual mothers and fathers to prepare now for the coming harvest. I believe that spiritual parenting is a God-designed development connected to the Great Commission and that we must embrace it to realize the full potential of the great harvest. I believe that mentoring is an important part of Jesus' strategy for the formation of disciples, and the investment in others will pay off great dividends of a multiplied spiritual inheritance.

Think about it: As a disciple maker, you can influence countless others and impact the world as you make an investment that keeps on growing. If you mentor one person who disciples another and if that one person disciples yet another and if each of those persons would each mentor one person, the effects of the multiplication would be astounding!

Are you ready to pour your resources into nurturing the spiritual strength of others? This kind of investment is most likely done without thanks and without any immediate ROI (return on investment). But God promises that when you invest, lives are changed. You have the opportunity to make an investment in someone's life that will not only have a significant impact on the world but also will last through eternity!

Key Questions for Practical Application

1. How do spiritual children become spiritual parents?
2. Why do you believe the Early Church multiplied rapidly?
3. In what specific ways can you prepare to reap the harvest as a disciple maker?

3

Becoming a Spiritual Family

Key: Spiritual parenting involves family-type relationships as a way of life.

More than 30 years ago, as young youth workers, my wife, La-Verne, and I began to develop what we then called Paul-Timothy discipling relationships with new Christians. I met with a few young men each week for Bible study and prayer and LaVerne did the same with a few young women. Early on, we realized these relationships were going to be works in progress, and it might be a long haul before we saw spectacular results. Many of the kids came from one particular neighborhood where gangs and drugs were problematic, and because most of the kids were first-generation believers, they received little support from friends and family.

We were young ourselves—we didn't know much and we made many mistakes, but our hearts were in the right place. After a short time, we knew that in order for these kids to grow spiritually and not fall away, we had to do more than spend time in a discipleship-type Bible study with them. They needed to see Christianity practically modeled and actually working, or none of it would make any sense to them. We didn't call it spiritual parenting, or spiritual mentoring, at the time, but we were do-ing it just the same. It was more than a duty or event for us—it was a lifestyle of being connected in relationships to younger Christians who desperately needed supportive, nurturing commitment from older Christians.

We opened our hearts and home to these kids and loved them unconditionally. Deep down we realized (though we weren't looking very far ahead at the time) that if we coached them to grow up spiritually, they could someday help others, and that would make every minute invested worth the effort.

So we welcomed these teenagers into our daily lives. They spent a lot of time hanging out at our house, creating permanent red Kool-Aid stains on the carpet and punching occasional holes in the wall during wrestling matches. Most of the training took place as they observed us lovingly disciplining our children or doing laundry or fixing that persistent leak in the roof. We learned step by step—with fits and starts—how to be effective spiritual parents, and they learned how to bear fruit as Christians.

The Lord was faithful: Out of our modest beginnings, a church was eventually birthed with some of those young believers who hung around our house, and they were trained to take on the next batch of spiritual children. Today through DOVE Christian Fellowship International, an international family of churches, we have the privilege of seeing many of our spiritual children, grandchildren and great-grandchildren reproduce spiritual sons and daughters as new small groups and hundreds of new churches are planted throughout the world.

There was nothing special about us—and there still isn't! We were ordinary young people who made lots of mistakes. To be certain, we have many stories that are not success stories, but we had the hearts of parents to teach our children. We loved Jesus, we really loved those kids, and, just like any parent, we expected our children to grow!

Research has shown that children learn best from observing and imitating behavior that is modeled. Mothers and fathers model acceptable behavior for their children, *leading* rather than *driving* them. Modern sheepherders often drive their flocks with the help of dogs, but the shepherds of ancient Israel walked ahead of the flock, and the sheep followed. God has revealed Himself to us as a Father, and He is calling fathers and mothers to follow His leading. Spiritual parents, in turn, are to model Christlike behavior and attitudes as their children follow after.

A Note About Gender and Age

Avoid the Possibility of Misinterpretation

Before we take a closer look at the hallmarks of spiritual mothers and fathers, it should be mentioned that it would be best if men should mentor men and women should mentor women, as modeled in Titus 2: "The older men [should] be sober, reverent, temperate, sound in faith. . . . Likewise exhort the young men to be sober-minded" (vv. 2-6, NKJV); "the older women likewise, that they be reverent in behavior, . . . teachers of good things—that they admonish the young women to love their husbands" (vv. 3-4, NKJV).

In counsel and example, the early Christian Church followed the parenting method of pairing older women with younger women and older men with younger men. There is a good reason for this. Fathering and mothering relationships fast become intimate friendships, and maintaining the boundaries of friendship between a man and a woman can be tricky. Deeply shared Christian love can be misinterpreted, leading to inappropriate emotional and physical attachments.

In my opinion, simply avoiding this trap is the best policy. "Abstain from all appearance of evil," says 1 Thessalonians 5:22 (KJV); in other words, "Avoid anything that could appear to reflect sin rather than uprightness." I believe it is entirely appropriate, however, for a husband and wife team to mentor a spiritual son or daughter together. In Acts 18:24-26, we read about the husband and wife team of Aquila and Priscilla, who helped enlighten Apollos concerning his knowledge of the gospel. Priscilla and Aquila "explained to him the way of God more adequately" (Acts 18:26).

Measure Maturity by Experience, Not Age

In contrast to gender, chronological age does not dictate the circumstance when someone can be a spiritual parent. You can be a spiritual parent when you are 16 and when you are 80. Between the ages of 12 and 16, all three of our daughters, Katrina, Charita and Leticia, became spiritual parents to younger girls in a small-group ministry. They took those kids under their wings and taught them simple biblical principles from God's Word. They prayed with them and cared for them when they had a need. Our daughters learned by *doing*. Out of their love for Jesus and those small girls, they took a step of obedience. They did not wait until they felt they were totally equipped; they became spiritual parents while they were still learning themselves.

After a seminar I once taught in Medford, Oregon, a young lady came up to me and thanked me for flying across the country to speak at her church. I asked her what the Lord was doing in her life. "Well," she said, "I have a few girls in school that I am meeting with each week to help them grow in their Christian lives." It was clear to me that she was a spiritual mother.

"How old are you?" I asked.

"Twelve," she replied. She was a spiritual mother at the age of 12! I meet many believers in their 50s and 60s who feel they cannot do what this 12-year-old has accepted as normal Christian living. What is wrong with this picture?

You can always find someone spiritually younger than you whom you can disciple and train in the ways of God, and soon that person will be ready to train someone else. The Bible's exhortation for older men to train younger men and older women to train younger women means that spiritual parents should be mature Christians who reflect *experience*. This does not necessarily mean an older-in-age woman needs to mentor a younger-in-age woman. *Age* has less to do with maturity than *experience*. Experience and spiritual maturity should be the yardstick that indicates who should mentor whom.

Regardless of age, the person's spiritual maturity is what qualifies him or her to instruct another. That means that a 20-year-old Christian male who is spiritually mature may be a spiritual father to a 50-year-old man who is new to the Christian faith. Recently I met for breakfast with a medical doctor who came to faith in Christ in his 40s. He spoke endearingly of a spiritual father in his life, much younger in age, who helped him grow in his newly found faith.

The younger-in-age spiritual father who instructs an older-in-age son may be the exception, however. More often, I believe the biblical mandate of spiritual mothering and fathering normally follows the pattern of chronological age. It is the older person with years of experience—the mature believer who has already been through many different seasons in life—who can most effectively disciple a younger person. Nevertheless, in both dynamics, the age differences work together to enrich the relationship, and it is clear that we need to learn how to release for reproduction spiritual parents of all ages.

The Love of a Mother

One day, nine-year-old Joey got off the bus from school and said, "Mom, the bus is so empty that we each could have our own seat, but those dumb girls all pile into one!" Joey's maleness could not comprehend the females' need to cluster.

God created men and women unique with respect to one another. The differences between men and women are meant to be a blessing and bring balance to life so that we can have a richer and fuller comprehension of the Father's love for us. Women seem to be programmed for intimacy and deep friendships and are often described as comforting, nurturing, intuitive and empathic. When women get together, they often talk about their feelings and their relationships, their work and their families; and their nurturing, mothering characteristics often come out as they communicate with each other. Women usually see themselves in relation to the people around them, preferring intimacy to separateness. This allows women to be uniquely in tune with close relationships.

The nurturing tendency in women is most evident in their capacity for love, which often goes beyond that of men. Proverbs 10:1 states, "A wise son brings joy to his father, but a foolish son grief to his mother." A mother usually feels deeper pain, because her love for her children is regarded as being more tender than a father's.

Of course, you don't have to be a biological mother to display tenderness and compassion. Any Christian woman who understands the heart of God and His everlasting love will develop nurturing, maternal characteristics. How do we know God has a tender, nurturing mother's heart? Time and time again in the holy Scriptures we get a picture of God's nurturing, mother-like tendencies: "Can a mother forget the baby at her breast and have no compassion on the child she has borne? Though she may forget, I will not forget you! See, I have engraved you on the palms of my hands" (Isa. 49:15-16). A little later in Isaiah, the Lord says, "As a mother comforts her child, so will I comfort you" (Isa. 66:13). God's deep, abiding love for us is greater than even that strongest of bonds: between a baby and his or her mother.

Another picture of God's nurturing and tender mother's heart is described by Christ when He showed His compassion for those who rejected Him: "O Jerusalem, Jerusalem, you who kill the prophets and stone those sent to you, how often I have longed to gather your children together, as a hen gathers her chicks under her wings, but you were not willing" (Matt. 23:37). Jesus longed to bestow His wonderful grace and favor onto all the spiritually blind in Jerusalem. Even though they refused His love, Jesus compassionately extended it, wanting to bring all of His people together just as a mother hen gathers her chicks for protection, safety, warmth and comfort under her wings.

The Mandate of Titus 2
As a young, 28-year-old pastor's wife, LaVerne struggled in the early days of ministry because of the pressure she felt to conform to the expected pastor's-wife role of organizing women's groups, meetings and programs. As she tells it, "I knew I was not going to be the typical pastor's wife who played the piano, organ or sang. I just did not feel called to be a public person. I knew God did not call me to spend my time heading committees and planning women's events. Every time I got down on my knees, I knew what God had called me to do. It was clear: Train a few women at a time."

So LaVerne spent the next few years doing just that. She started to pour her life into a few of the women who were small-group leaders in the church. It wasn't a job for the fainthearted! The relationships she developed took time and effort. She was not standing up front, basking in the applause of an adoring public.

For years, she trained women behind the scenes. She loved them as she inquired how their marriages were faring. She prayed and wept with them as they went through life's hard spots and rejoiced with them when they experienced life's joys. Those women were equipped to pass on to other women the impartation they had received from LaVerne. The results have been a multiplication of LaVerne's initial efforts with a few women.

Today, LaVerne continues to parent women one on one. And when she speaks to larger crowds, she frequently hears individual young women cry out, "But where are the older women? Where is that spiritual mother who will come alongside me and help me grow up in my Christian life?" With tears streaming down her face, each younger woman seems to say, "Sometimes I could just use an hour of a spiritually mature woman's time. I so desperately need to be encouraged to look to the Father. I need to hear from someone who has spiritual maturity beyond mine and can teach me valuable lessons from her own experience. I need someone to tell me I am going to make it during this season of my life—that I'll make it to the end of the week!" Women are looking for friends, coaches, cheerleaders who can point them to Jesus.

I believe the Lord is calling Christian women to obey His call today to take spiritual daughters under their wings. Christian women need spiritual mothers to help them grow into healthy women of God. Spiritual mothers walk alongside other women, put their arms around their daughters and say, "You can make it!" Susan Hunt, the former director of women's ministries for the Presbyterian Church of America, writes in her book *Spiritual Mothering* that spiritual mothering is "when a woman possessing faith and spiritual maturity enters into a nurturing relationship with a younger woman in order to encourage and equip her to live for God's glory."[1]

God's Word gives women a clear mandate and model for spiritual mothering. Paul told Titus how to set up spiritual parenting relationships, and into this context he exhorted older women to put their energies into training and teaching younger women:

> [Teach] the older women . . . that they be reverent in behavior, not slanderers, not given to much wine, teachers of good things—that they admonish the younger women to love their husbands, to love their children, to be discreet, chaste, homemakers, good, obedient to their husbands, that the word of God may not be blasphemed (Titus 2:3-5, *NKJV*).

Paul knew the Church would be impacted if older women would start teaching younger women by their godly lifestyles. If mature women will give of themselves and invest their energies in younger women, the Kingdom will be advanced. God wants to use women who revere (fear) God, who are free from slander and who are not captive to addictive behaviors. These mature women are ready to be spiritual mothers.

Spiritually mature women unselfishly give of themselves. They submit their wills to God and to His leadership. Out of love for Him, they have learned the secret of Philippians 2:3-4: "Let nothing be done through selfish ambition or conceit, but in lowliness of mind let each esteem others better than [herself]. Let each of you look out not only for [your] own interests, but also for the interests of others" (*NKJV*). Spiritually mature women are not absorbed by their own concerns but unselfishly look out for the needs of others.

The Challenge of Spiritual Mothering

Remember that it is the character of Christ that qualifies an individual to be a spiritual mother. Potential spiritual mothers must be women who fear God. This means they need to care more about what God thinks of them than what other people think. Suffering from a poor self-image will hinder spiritual mothering. There are pressures in life to conform and act certain ways, but when the fear of God comes over a woman, she asks God what *He* thinks of her. She knows that Christ accepts her because of His blood and that His is an unconditional love. This brings freedom into her life.

LaVerne was speaking at a women's retreat about God's unconditional love, and a woman who had been a Christian for a long time came up to her and said, "I don't think I understand God's unconditional love. Growing up, I felt love from my parents only when I performed satisfactorily for them. So I've always put conditions on my love when I related to others." That day, she acknowledged her wrong thinking and chose to accept God's unfathomable, unconditional love for her. Her life was changed! God loves individuals whether they perform or not. His love is extended without conditions. When God's people understand this, they will minister to others, not out of duty to them, but out of His love for them. It is through this love that we serve one another (see Gal. 5:13).

Another thing that will hinder spiritual mothering is selfishness. "I'm too busy," "I've raised my children," "I'm retired—just let me relax by the ocean" are all selfish excuses for not investing in the growth of a spiritual daughter. Several years ago, at 48 years of age and after raising seven children of her own, one of LaVerne's spiritual mothers, Naomi, took in a young foster son. Then her elderly mother moved in with her family. Some would probably look at Naomi and say, "Isn't it time to take a break and ease up?" But by getting a babysitter for her son and elderly mother at home, this dedicated spiritual mother still made time to get together with LaVerne.

And her commitment has made a lasting impression on LaVerne: "When I feel lazy and want to gripe and complain," says LaVerne, "I just can't make excuses for myself, because I have a spiritual mom in my life who doesn't have it easy but chooses to walk in joy."

It takes a special kind of grace to be a mother—either a natural mother or a spiritual one—in today's world. Being a mother is not easy. There is a huge emotional investment along with the physical exertion of the 24-hours-a-day demand required for motherhood. A woman who understands this is willing to admit her total dependence on the grace of the Lord.

Although it is important for women to have loving and nurturing one-on-one relationships, these relationships must hinge on the more important vertical relationship with God. Every spiritual mother-daughter relationship needs to focus on glorifying God and yielding to His will and purpose. In the kitchen of a mother I know hangs a plaque that reads, "The greatest thing a mother can do for her children is to love their father." You could paraphrase that adage to say, "The greatest thing a spiritual mother can do for her spiritual children is to love her heavenly Father!" The entire focus of the relationship must be to glorify God.

This point is brought out clearly in the first chapter of Luke, where we learn about the interaction between Elizabeth and Mary. Elizabeth and Mary had a lot in common: For one, they both had unusual pregnancies! When Mary came to visit Elizabeth, they could have focused on their unique situations and talked about all they were feeling, empathizing with each other and calling attention to their own needs. Instead, upon greeting each other, their focus was *upward*. Their relationship was not based on what they needed from each other. Elizabeth, like a seasoned spiritual mother, encouraged Mary, who, in turn, burst forth in praise to God:

> And it happened, when Elizabeth heard the greeting of Mary, that the babe leaped in her womb; and Elizabeth was filled with the Holy Spirit. Then she spoke out with a loud voice and said, "Blessed are you among women, and blessed is the fruit of your womb! But why is this granted to me, that the mother of my Lord should come to me? For indeed, as soon as the voice of your greeting sounded in my ears, the babe leaped in my womb for joy. Blessed is she who believed, for there will be a fulfillment of those things which were told her from the Lord."
>
> And Mary said: "My soul magnifies the Lord, and my spirit has rejoiced in God my Savior. For He has regarded the lowly state of His maidservant; for behold, henceforth all generations will call me blessed. For He who is mighty has done great things for me, and holy is His name" (Luke 1:41-49, *NKJV*).

The purpose of a spiritual mothering relationship is to glorify God. He is your hope: "Christ in you, the hope of glory" (Col. 1:27). What an awesome concept: Christ, the anointed One, lives within you! It is Christ who ministers through you. It's not about what you do for God but about what God does in and through you. *He* does the spiritual mothering through you as you yield to Him.

The Father of the Family

Family has long been God's idea. He ordained and designed it: "I will be a Father to you, and you will be my sons and daughters, says the Lord Almighty" (2 Cor. 6:18). The apostle Paul's affectionate prayer for his beloved Ephesians reflects this idea as well: "For this reason I kneel before the Father, from whom his whole family in heaven and on earth derives its name" (Eph. 3:14-15). God is the Father of an entire great family, which includes all those who name Jesus Christ as Lord. He is the Father from whom all fatherhood derives its meaning and inspiration. We have to understand *His* Fatherhood—His love, forgiveness and acceptance—if we are to understand healthy family relationships.

Unfortunately, many in today's generation have a warped understanding of fatherhood, because many fathers have abused their authority or been absent, causing a breach of trust and a lack of security. With poor role models in the world, God's people—the Church of Jesus Christ—must stand in the gap created by missing or cruel fathers to model God's intention for family.

"The church must begin to understand its role as a parenting influence—as a holistic life-growth community," says my friend Robert Stearns in his book *Prepare the Way*. This is what Stearns, a worldwide influential minister and Christian bridge builder, sees happening when we begin to understand that parenting role:

> God will lead many men who have the Father's heart to
> begin to mentor young men in their congregations. . . .
> Older women will take the younger under their wings and
> impart love, nurturing, and wisdom. Strong families will

reach out to single-parent homes and welcome ongoing
interaction between the families, bringing strength and
combating the overwhelming sense of "aloneness." . . .
We will move toward the joy that the early Church exuded
as they lived in fellowship with each other and the Lord.[2]

What an incredible picture! And it will become reality when
we realize that we can no longer live independently of each other.
God wants to restore fathering and mothering to His kingdom,
and it starts with His promise to be a Father to us. But for believers to experience true family life, fathers must assume their
responsibility as spiritual parents.

Fathers bring strength, stability and balance to the family.
A natural father is meant to be a protector, counselor and guide
to his children so that they can grow up secure in their father's
love and guidance. If they lack a healthy father role model, children cannot achieve their full potential as healthy individuals.
According to Dr. David Cannistraci, author and seasoned pastor,
healthy fathering is essential to success at every level of society:

Sociologists are now confirming that fathers not only
play an indispensable role in the home, but also in the
nation. Many of the problems we face in America today—
drugs, welfare, teenage pregnancy—are directly related
to the absence of fathers throughout the past several
decades. . . . Spiritual fatherlessness is a weakness in the
Body of Christ today; a great vacuum has been created by
the scarcity of godly fathering. Like society, the Church
is plagued with problems. We need the same kind of discipline and accountability a natural father brings to a
natural family. We need wisdom and maturity, a firm
hand to guide us, balance to preserve us and experience
to comfort us.[3]

Statistics today show a society with an alarming trend toward
the deterioration of the family. Marriages are failing, parents
are absent—and children are paying the emotional, financial,

physical and spiritual consequences. A popular view some years ago was that external forces—such as street crime, bad schools and economic stress—were the culprits of the crises in family life. Today's critics challenge this view. The revised thinking is that it is the breakdown of families that feeds these and other social ills. Therefore, it is only as we reclaim the family that our society can in turn be healed:

> While many voices are crying out that we need more government to protect our families, the church is responding to a different voice—the voice of a Father. God has revealed Himself as our Father, and He is calling fathers within the church to follow His example.[4]

Similarities Between a Spiritual Father and a Natural Father

"There are at least five similarities between a spiritual father and a natural father," according to pastor, author and community leader Dr. David Cannistraci.[5] And if we understand these similarities—these functions—we can begin to follow the model of the Father, as well as nurture these characteristics in the next generation of spiritual parents:

1. *Fathers demonstrate love.* The love relationship between a father and his children provides the ideal environment for training and developing the characters and lives of the children. Without love, children may grow but cannot flourish. Fathers affirm their children and provide the gentle security of an unwavering commitment to their wellbeing.

2. *Fathers train and discipline.* Fathers take a powerful part in firmly directing and guiding their children into activities and attitudes that will prepare them for success. True fathers accept responsibility for their children. The biblical role of fathers is to raise their children to a place of maturity and fruitfulness.

3. *Fathers provide.* To provide means to sustain and enrich. What do spiritual fathers provide for their spiritual children? An inheritance of God's blessing. A legacy of spirit comes from spiritual fathers to their spiritual children.

4. *Fathers reproduce.* In the most basic sense, natural fathers are men who have physically contributed to creating a new life. Spiritual fathers give spiritual life to new children in the faith by becoming the vessels through which those children enter into new birth. They continue their ministries as fathers by raising up and reproducing their own ministries within those lives.

5. *Fathers bless and impart.* Many fathers understand well how to love, provide for and train their children, but many lack the ability that the great apostolic fathers of the Early Church profitably exercised: imparting spiritual blessing. The apostle Paul pictured God the Father blessing us as His children with all spiritual blessings through our relationship with Christ (see Eph. 1:3). Paul laid his hands on his spiritual son, Timothy, and was used to impart gifts and blessings that Timothy was responsible to utilize (see 2 Tim. 1:6). This transference of divine life is one of the most awesome responsibilities of a spiritual father. Speaking from experience, I can say that this is one of the greatest experiences any spiritual son can have.

The Rebuilding of Trust in Fathers

If the hearts of fathers are not restored to their children—both natural and spiritual—Malachi 4:6 states that the Lord will "strike the land with a curse." When relationships between the generations are estranged, they are—quite literally—cursed. God's desire is to take a generation that has been cursed by this breakdown of family relationships and to rebuild trust. God's Son, Jesus, came to restore broken relationships—the relationship between the Father and humankind and the relationship between fathers and children. This family connection is a means for blessing and restoration between the generations.

Trust is often broken in today's society, because parents have neglected their children at the expense of their own happiness or agendas. Children are left vulnerable in the wake of a divorce as they are shuttled between conflicting and sometimes hostile parents; and they often become frustrated, confused and insecure. This same kind of curse can exist between spiritual parents and their estranged spiritual children. Church leaders have often been so busy with their programs and committees that they have no time to train spiritual children to become future spiritual parents. This is a blight on the Church, stunting future generations of leaders.

I've heard it said that children should forgive their parents for being less than perfect, and parents should work hard to make sure their children have as little to forgive as possible. If the damage has already been done, both natural children and spiritual children must reach a place of maturity where they can forgive their neglectful parents, or they will grow up angry and distrustful.

Our God wants to convict of neglect natural fathers and spiritual fathers who have been irresponsible and caught up in their own agendas. God alone is the One who can repair the damage and reconnect fathers to their lonely children. Fathers must repent of their self-seeking and carelessness and begin the long process of rebuilding their children's trust. The Lord wants to restore relationships between the young and the old so that a powerful spiritual legacy can not only persevere but also proliferate.

Differences Between Spiritual Parenting Women and Men

Why is it that women trust other women so much more readily than men trust other men? How can women enter a room and almost immediately begin to open up and be vulnerable about their lives and their families while the men open up about last night's game or last week's fishing expedition? Do women respond differently to parenting than men? I propose that there needs to be no difference; but, yes, most women seem to easily form relationships that lend themselves to deep spiritual parenting, while most men struggle to do so. It's not wrong—it's simply different.

Women seem to be created to naturally gravitate toward the vulnerability that spiritual parenting relationships are built on. It takes a little more convincing for men. Men need to see a worthwhile purpose, a beginning and an end, a goal to shoot for and a response from the ones receiving our gifts of time. Men want to know that these relationships are making a difference and have tangible, measurable results. They have adapted to certain rules in relationships, and these rules are hard to breach: Don't trust unless the relationship has proven trustworthy. Don't be too vulnerable too soon. Watch for the level of energy expended in this relationship as compared to the results observed. Watch the level of personal involvement (that is, don't care too much).

While men are hungry for friendship, psychologist Dr. Ken Druck says:

> We will not allow ourselves to get together with male friends because we enjoy their company. It is not "safe" simply to want some male companionship. We have to legitimize the feeling. We have to throw in a card game, a ball game, or some beer to make the occasion a "safe" one.[6]

Prayer, however, breaks down the barriers and exposes the heart. Praying together is the key that most often unlocks the ability for anyone to share his or her innermost feelings. This is especially true of men.

Spiritual fathers (and, of course, mothers) must come to peace with who they are. Spiritual parenthood is not based on what the spiritual parents need. Too often we gravitate to what we feel we should be receiving, but this approach will skew the relationship from the starting blocks. Men must put to rest their preconceived ideas about the personal gains or benefits from their spiritual children. The reward is mostly eternal, yet even that "personal gain" must be far from men's minds.

There are many times the spiritual fathering relationship may feel—and in fact is—one-sided. After all, why not? As a spiritual father, I am responsible to be the initiator: the initiator of the phone calls, the initiator of the get-togethers, the initiator of prayer, the initiator of studying a book or the Bible. I am the initiator. There is no room for such thoughts as, *I called him last time*, or, *If he cared about this relationship, he would pay for breakfast.*

I am not asking men to respond to spiritual parenting like most women do, but I think it is important to identify some of the hurdles that men will undoubtedly face in this type of relationship. The goal is not to become feminized but to become like Jesus, who was the all-time best spiritual Father who ever walked the earth. If Jesus was capable of transcending His maleness and closely connect with His disciples, then so can we. (More about the Jesus model of spiritual parenting in chapter 9.)

The heavenly Father made men and women different and declared of those differences, "It is good" (see Gen. 1:31). The truth is, we need both genders to rise to their full potential to parent more and more generations of healthy spiritual children.

The Duties of Parents

Parents Are Servants

Before you can be a spiritual mother or father, you must first check your motives. Spiritual parenting is a behind-the-scenes kind of deal. It's not likely that someone will pat you on the back and say, "What a good job you're doing. Keep up the good work!" Why? Because being a parent is not something you *do* as much as it is someone you *are*. I don't have to tell people I'm a father. They know it when they meet my son and my three daughters.

Scripture warns us about giving ourselves impressive titles in an effort to try to gain the honor and respect of others: "And do not call anyone on earth 'father,' for you have one Father, and he is in heaven. . . . The greatest among you will be your servant"

(Matt. 23:9,11). The apostle Paul called himself a father several times in Scripture, but he used the word "father" "to denote, not authority, but affection: therefore he calls them not his *obliged*, but his *beloved*, sons (1 Cor. 4:14)."[7]

The measure of the greatness of a spiritual father or a spiritual mother is always the measure of his or her servanthood and love.

Parents Love and Encourage Their Children

Spiritual parents love and gently encourage their children to move in the right direction as they progress on their journeys. Paul the apostle showed how much he, as a spiritual parent, loved the Thessalonian believers: "We were gentle among you, like a mother caring for her little children. We loved you so much that we were delighted to share with you not only the gospel of God but our lives as well, because you had become so dear to us" (1 Thess. 2:7-8). Like a nursing mother, tender and gentle, Paul cherished the people he had fathered spiritually. When spiritual children are impacted with a parent's affection, they know it and respond in an upright manner.

With mature spiritual parents at their sides, children will grow strong and learn quickly and naturally by example. Parents teach, train, set good examples and provide role models. Spiritual parents raise the awareness of attitudes or behaviors in their children's lives that need to be changed for the better and help them take an honest look at their lives and make adjustments so that their actions and behaviors can improve. It's only when spiritual children know that they are loved and accepted that they have the confidence they need to make changes and hard choices.

Parents Expect Their Children to Grow

Parents expect their children to grow up in every way—physically, spiritually, mentally and emotionally. Through the natural progression of time and with much love and the right amount of training, children are expected to mature into healthy adults and move out to start homes of their own.

Twenty-one years after having our first child, I walked down the aisle with my "baby" girl at my side on her wedding day. I realized I had spent all those years of time, effort and money just to give her away to her fiancé! We had raised her to give her away. She and her husband now have three children of their own, and they have the opportunity to be spiritual parents and prepare the next generation. Parenting is all about passing on a legacy. Spiritual parenting involves a whole package of loving, training, modeling, imparting and multiplying—all with the expectation that your children will grow up to begin the cycle again.

In the book of Colossians, we read about how Paul modeled fatherhood to Epaphras when he made himself available in a time of need. It seems that Epaphras had been converted and carried the gospel to Colossae. Because of his previous relationship to Paul, Epaphras came to Rome to seek Paul's seasoned counsel about the errors that then threatened the Colossian church. In response, Paul wrote his letter to the Colossians, a letter from a father who cared deeply. Paul could write this fathering letter because he felt a stewardship for the people through his relationship with Epaphras (see Col. 1:7-8). Parents who model parenthood like this perpetuate a legacy through their sons and daughters as they, in turn, learn how to parent others into the Kingdom.

My friend Peter Bunton, well experienced in world missions and church leadership, has years of experience training and mentoring young people. He has this to say about nurturing spiritual children to maturity:

> A spiritual father or mother should be prepared to father or mother those of different personalities and gifts. Sometimes a very different mentor is needed to help spiritual sons or daughters learn other facets of their ministry. A test of a spiritual father's security is whether he can help someone more gifted than himself!

I agree with Peter. It is a common desire of natural parents to see greatness in their children, a greatness that will make God's world a better place. Likewise, a spiritual parent should expect and desire his or her spiritual children to go far beyond him or her spiritually. Whether the spiritual child already has many gifts or receives a new impartation through the parent's example, a spiritual father or mother's greatest joy should be to see his or her children succeed.

Parents Set an Example for Their Children

In order to grow in God, people need someone to speak truth into their lives and model what walking in faith means. "Remember your leaders, who spoke the word of God to you. Consider the outcome of their way of life and imitate their faith" (Heb. 13:7). If spiritual fathers and mothers present true and godly examples of what it means to live by faith to those they serve, their spiritual daughters and sons will gladly imitate them. This initiates a legacy of spiritual parenting.

In 1 Thessalonians 2:11, Paul reminds that church that he set an example as a father, exhorting, comforting and charging each believer "as a father deals with his own children." Spiritual fathers and mothers are models to emulate so that younger Christians can grow up to be nurturing, caring and encouraging adults and eventually capable, healthy parents themselves. It's no secret that children reared in healthy, loving families grow up to be healthy, loving parents. Providing an example for others to imitate and reproduce is an important aspect of spiritual parenting.

Parents Give Children a Sense of Significance

One goal of parents is to build a healthy sense of self-worth in their children. In his book *Seven Things Children Need*, pastor and seminary teacher John Drescher says that every child wants to be noticed and recognized as a person of worth:

> It is almost impossible to live with ourselves if we feel we are of little value or if we don't like ourselves. . . . A person who feels like a nobody will contribute little to life. This needs to be stressed here because the great plague of inferiority feelings starts early in life. We human beings

need to be noticed, appreciated, and loved as we are, if we are to have a sense of significance.[8]

Leaders often become leaders only when someone believes in them as leaders. Years ago, there was a young believer in our small group who felt as if he could not pray in public. Keith admitted he felt inadequate among all the more mature Christians whose prayers came easily. I did not give him a formula to follow, but I saw potential in him and encouraged him to step out of his comfort zone. One day, Keith urged me, "Ask me to pray sometime when I'm not expecting it." I was happy to oblige! Very soon at a small-group meeting, I asked Keith to begin our prayer session with a one-sentence prayer. It was a place to start, and Keith prayed because I believed he could do it. My trust in him helped him to overcome his feelings of inadequacy. He went on to assume leadership in a small group and later served as a deacon in his local church.

Spiritual children will grow in responsibility and achievement when someone believes in them. Parents must see their children in the light of who they can become.

Parents Offer a Place of Safety for Their Children

God wants to provide relationships where spiritual mothers and fathers contribute a sense of protection to their spiritual children so that they can mature in their Christian lives. As parents, we want to protect our natural children from the madness around them. We want them to know that however terrible the world becomes, they can find comfort and shelter in a God who cares deeply for them and wants them to take risks and succeed.

In the same way, spiritual children must feel safe to make mistakes and to take shelter from the world's ills. Spiritual children need protection, nurturing, care, guidance and encouragement from their spiritual parents.

The Definition of a Spiritual Parent

Spiritual fathers and mothers might be called mentors or coaches or disciplers, because they help their daughters and sons negotiate the obstacles of their spiritual journeys. A coach is someone who wants to see you win. A coach tells you that you *can* make it. My favorite definition of a spiritual parent can be simply stated:

> A spiritual father or mother helps a spiritual son or daughter reach his or her God-given potential.

It is that uncomplicated and that profound. Bobb Biehl, a master of mentoring and leadership development, describes mentoring this way: "Mentoring is more 'how can I help you?' than 'what should I teach you?'"[9]

Of course, spiritual parents *do* teach spiritual truths, but their energies often are focused on caring for and helping those they mentor in the many different aspects of their lives. Spiritual parenting relationships cannot be formal relationships involved in only teaching because, by definition and by practice, parenthood is informal interaction. It takes place along the highways and byways of life. Parenthood is a lifestyle.

Key Questions for Practical Application

1. What is the Titus 2 Mandate and how does it relate to the life of a spiritual mother?
2. What are some similarities between natural and spiritual fathers?
3. What positive impact has spiritual parenting had on your life?

Growing to Spiritual Parenthood

Key: There are three stages of growth for every believer.

Somehow many of us have been duped into thinking that spiritual maturity can be attained only by super saints who pray five hours a day, attend church four times a week and follow a vigorous Bible-reading program. And we despair when we don't measure up. While it is true that as we mature spiritually, we will find ourselves wanting to read the Bible more often and pray more frequently; but growing to maturity happens in much more practical and gradual ways. I believe growth happens especially as we reach out to the less spiritually mature, rather than constantly needing to be fed ourselves. Maturity requires that we become more responsible for others.

Growing from a spiritual baby into a spiritual parent is crucial to God's divine order. That's why God established a natural training ground for us—stages through which we grow to parenthood. According to the Bible, these three growth stages are (1) child, (2) young man (or woman), and (3) father (or mother). At each point in our journeys, we function in a particular way and have distinct tasks to perform. John addresses all three spiritual stages in 1 John 2:12-14:

> I write to you, dear children, because your sins have been forgiven on account of his name. I write to you, fathers,

because you have known him who is from the beginning. I write to you, young men, because you have overcome the evil one. I write to you, dear children, because you have known the Father. I write to you, fathers, because you have known him who is from the beginning. I write to you, young men, because you are strong, and the word of God lives in you, and you have overcome the evil one.

International speaker, teacher and spiritual father Alan Vincent from San Antonio, Texas, shared this in a note to me about these verses in 1 John:

The cry of the apostle John was not only for strong men who knew the Word of God and could overcome the evil one, but for *fathers* who really knew God and who would come forth to father the church. If men as a whole became strong fathers according to the biblical pattern—in home, church and society—then most of our social problems would disappear and Satan's kingdom would be severely curtailed. Fatherhood is the foundation on which God has chosen to build the whole structure of society.

Children must grow up. They become spiritual young women and men by having the Word of God living in them and by overcoming the assaults of the devil. In turn, as young people grow into maturity and develop an intimate relationship with God, they become spiritual mentors, or parents—and in order to become spiritual parents, they need to have spiritual children!

If we fail to take the natural steps of becoming spiritual young men and women and then becoming spiritual parents, we remain babies—spiritually immature and lacking parenting skills. It is sad, but this scenario is often the case in the Church. Many times there are no provisions within our Church systems to help believers develop and mature. Sometimes people simply do not want to take the responsibility of becoming spiritual parents. They may feel that they are too busy or they fear that they will be burned out by someone they are mentoring. They may feel that they have little to offer, because they don't feel mature enough themselves. Whatever reason people may give, I believe it is still God's best for everyone to be given the opportunity to do the work of ministry and connect in vital relationships with others. Through modeling and impartation, spiritual reproduction *does* happen.

Spiritual Children

Natural babies bring new life to a family! They laugh and cry, expressing their needs immediately and freely. They are self-centered— they do not know any better, and we gladly supply their needs. Parents don't mind when babies mess in their diapers, because that's what babies do. Although their fussing and crying may interfere with the parents' schedules, Mom and Dad are happy to care for their child because the child is little and defenseless and needs help. Caring parents would never deny their child their attention.

Spiritual babies in the Body of Christ are wonderful, too! And good spiritual parents are happy to spend extra time with spiritual children in order to steer them in the right direction. Similar to natural babies, spiritual children need constant assurance and care and often do the unexpected, because they are still learning what following Jesus means. According to 1 John 2:12, they are "children" whose "sins have been forgiven," which puts them in fellowship with God and other believers. And that's their focus: forgiveness of sins, getting to heaven and learning to know the Father. Like natural babies, they know their Father, though it is probably not a thorough knowledge of God. Spiritual children are most aware of and alive to what they can receive from the One who saved them. They freely ask the Father when they have a need. Have you ever noticed how new believers can pray prayers that seem theologically unsound, yet God answers almost every one? The Father is quick to take care of these little ones.

The Problem of Arrested Development

What happens when spiritual babies do not grow up? Men and women who still have childish emotions, toddler angers and adolescent behaviors well into their adult years are described by psychologists as having arrested development. Those whose development is arrested have simply stopped growing emotionally and are stuck in an immature stage in life. And let's be honest: However endearing children are when they are young, childishness quickly loses its appeal when it does not pass with time. A childish adult is not attractive. Neither is a believer who has not grown up spiritually.

A pastor friend of mine lamented, "Sometimes I feel like I have to walk down the aisles each Sunday to give everyone their spiritual bottles. And what really bothers me is that I have to part the whiskers of some of the spiritual babies to give them their bottles!"

In other words, it's not only new believers who are spiritual babies in the Church today. Older Christians who lack spiritual maturity are adults in chronological age but babies in spiritual growth. They may be 20 years old, 40, 60 or even older—believers for many years—but never have spiritually matured. They live self-centered lifestyles, complaining and fussing and throwing temper tantrums when things don't go their way. Some may not accept the fact that God loves them for who they are. Others may wallow in self-pity when they fail. Still others may live under an immense cloud of guilt and condemnation.

Maybe you are familiar with the story about a little boy named Matthew whose mother put him to bed one night and then went back downstairs. About 30 minutes later she heard a thump on the floor. She knew exactly what had happened—he had fallen out of bed. She went upstairs and found Matthew sitting in the middle of the floor, looking bewildered. She asked, "Matthew, what happened?"

He said, "I don't know. I guess I just stayed too close to where I got in."

There are spiritual children who have stayed too close to where they got in. They desperately need to grow up so that they can become spiritual young women and men and eventually spiritual parents.

Steps to Move Spiritual Children to Maturity

New believers often act like natural children, with all the ensuing marks of immaturity, including instability and gullibility. Like natural babies, they may be self-centered, selfish and irresponsible, but spiritual parents know that eventually their spiritual children will grow up. In time, they will mature as they grow into a loving relationship with Jesus Christ. Good spiritual parents focus on teaching the early lessons of Christian faith and moving those they mentor on to new horizons. They know that growing people constantly reach out for maturity in personhood and personality.

To move their spiritual children on to the next stage of maturity, spiritual fathers and mothers should take the following specific steps:

1. *Teach the spiritual children the Word of God.* Do this either one on one or in a small-group setting where everyone is learning the same basic foundational teachings. (I suggest using the 12-book Biblical Foundation Series that I have written for this purpose.[1])

2. *Realize that new believers need more care than those who are more spiritually mature.* In the same way a stake is placed next to a growing tree to give it stability and support as it begins to grow, new believers need mature believers to stake them—to stand with them—as they begin their new lives in Christ.

3. *Get the new believers involved with other believers in both small-group and large-group settings.* Providing spiritual children with both types of experiences will prevent their becoming emotionally dependent on their spiritual mother or father.

4. *Involve the spiritual children in day-to-day living situations.* New believers need to see the faith lived out before them. This means that spiritual parents should involve those they mentor in such mundane tasks as going to a store or watching a football game. In other words, spiritual parents should allow their spiritual children to see them in real-life situations.

Spiritual Young Women and Men

Spiritual babies need to be spoon-fed, but spiritual young women and men have learned to feed themselves as they meditate on the

Word of God. They have grown to the next stage, but they still have some growing up to do. Whether they are young adults in chronological age or spiritual age, they are not yet mature enough to instruct others; however, they *are* developing, and their youthful enthusiasm and idealism are potent forces. Spiritual young adults are often able to see the simple truth of a complicated matter and are able to work tirelessly for a good cause. Fearless and strong, they bring zeal to the Body of Christ.

According to 1 John 2:14, young women and men are strong with God's Word in their hearts, and they have won their struggles against Satan. They don't need to run to others in the Church to care for them like spiritual babies do, because they have learned how to apply the Word to their own lives. When the devil tempts them, they know what to do to overcome him. They use the Word of God effectively and powerfully!

Paul gives this advice to Timothy, his young friend and spiritual son: "Don't let anyone look down on you because you are young, but set an example for the believers in speech, in life, in love, in faith and in purity" (1 Tim. 4:12). Timothy was young in age, but Paul fathered him until he determined that he was spiritually mature and ready to be a spiritual father in his own right. Like Timothy, spiritual young men and women are strong in the Word and Spirit. They have learned to use the strengths of spiritual discipline, of prayer and of the study of the Word. They are alive to what they can do for Jesus, and one day soon, under the guidance of their spiritual mothers and fathers, they will be spiritual parents.

The Trap of Youthful Temptations

Spiritual parents must be aware that although spiritual young women and men are headed in the right direction, the temptations of youth may be a trap for those who have not yet developed a strong sense of right and wrong. Paul knew that Timothy, as a young person in chronological age, was subject to the same passions as other young people. He warned him to "run from anything that gives you the evil thoughts that young men often have" (2 Tim. 2:22, *TLB*). Spiritual young men and women must be cautioned to run from youthful passions that could lead to sin.

When I was eight years old, I thought my daddy knew everything. When I turned 13, I thought, *There are a few things this man doesn't know!* When I got to be 16 years of age, there were times when I thought, *My father is prehistoric!* Then in my early 20s I got married, and a few years later we had our first child. I was shocked to discover all my father had learned in those intervening years!

You know what happened: *I* was the one who had changed. I had matured and realized my dad knew much more than I had thought he did. Parenthood had tempered me. Today I think of my father as one of the wisest men I have ever known.

Spiritual young women and men can easily become arrogant and dogmatic. After returning from Bible college or from a short-term missions experience or after having read the latest faith-based book, they may think they have all the answers. They are not yet tempered by parenthood. It's only by becoming spiritual fathers and mothers—by really experiencing spiritual parenthood's joys and disciplines—that they can be tempered.

Steps to Develop Spiritual Maturity

Spiritual parents must do everything they can to encourage spiritual young women and men to develop their ministries while they are still young, to become spiritual parents as soon as they are ready. To do so, spiritual mothers and fathers should take a few specific steps:

1. *Give the spiritual young women and men small areas of spiritual responsibility.* For example, ask them if they are comfortable to lead in prayer in a small group.

2. *Ask the spiritual young women and men to pray a short prayer of faith as the parents pray for healing for someone who is sick and needs prayer.*

3. *Ask the spiritual young adults to organize once or twice a time of fellowship with others when the parents need not be in attendance.*

4. *Ask the spiritual young adults to pray daily for someone in their small group or local church.* This will encourage them to develop and grow spiritually.

> 5. *Encourage the spiritual young women and men to share,*
> *with both believers and unbelievers, their "God Story," de-*
> *scribing how they came to faith.*

Spiritual Mothers and Fathers

Susan, a young mother and a new believer, joined one of her church's small groups, expecting to learn biblical values and spend time with fellow Christians. But something much greater happened. Liz, an older woman in the group, asked Susan if she wanted to spend one-on-one time together for extra encouragement and accountability.

Of course, Susan was thrilled. Liz was such a spiritual giant in Susan's eyes! Susan expected that she would listen as Liz taught her all she needed to know about living a victorious Christian life. Not only did Liz know God's Word, but she also was the most compassionate woman Susan had ever met!

Susan's first surprise was that Liz was so low-key when they first met together away from the small group. She didn't lecture Susan or act superspiritual. Second, it soon become apparent that Liz really loved her, as a mother loves her daughter. Bit by bit, Susan opened up her heart to Liz, who was easy to talk to, because she was transparent in sharing about her own struggles in her marriage, job and family. She taught Susan how to rely on Scripture for answers, and she prayed with Susan about everything.

Liz generously and selflessly poured out her life, and Susan blossomed spiritually. A new Christian was brought to maturity because she had a Christlike role model. The spiritual growth happened easily and naturally as she experienced the love and patience of a spiritual parent. Now Susan, having learned through Liz's modeling, has taken the step to become a spiritual parent herself.

The Single Step to Take to Become Spiritual Parents

Just how do spiritual young people grow up to become spiritual mothers and fathers? There is only one way—to have children! You could memorize the entire book of Leviticus and repeat it backward while standing on your head, but your knowledge and expertise would not make you a spiritual mother or father. Spiritual parents become parents by having spiritual children. It is as simple as that!

A spiritually mature Christian can become a spiritual parent either by spiritual adoption (parenting someone who is already a believer but who needs mentoring) or by spiritual new birth (parenting someone you have personally led to Christ). Onesimus was a spiritual son to Paul by being born again, while Timothy was a spiritual son by adoption. Paul led Onesimus to Christ while he (Paul) was in prison (see Philem. 10). Paul met Timothy while in Lystra after Timothy had come to Christ earlier under the influence of his mother and grandmother (see Acts 16:1-3; 2 Tim. 1:5). Paul treated both adopted son Timothy and reborn son Onesimus as his spiritual sons and was committed to helping them mature spiritually. And he called both of them son (see, for example, 1 Tim. 1:2; Philem. 10).

Spiritual parents are mature believers who have grown and matured in their Christian walk and are ready to invest in the growth and maturity of others. They are called fathers (or mothers), according to 1 John 2:13: "I write to you, fathers, because you have known him who is from the beginning." This implies a profound and thorough knowledge of Jesus through His Word. It also implies a deep sense of passionate acquaintance with Him through His Holy Spirit. Mature Christians are awake to their calling to be like Jesus—to be spiritual mentors as modeled by God's Son. They understand what it takes to be spiritual parents and are willing to become spiritual parents.

Steps to Take to Grow as Spiritual Parents

I will never forget the experience of becoming a father for the first time. I faithfully attended prenatal classes where I learned how to coach LaVerne through her labor. After only three sessions, the nurse told us she would see us at the hospital. Scary.

When the contractions started, reality hit me and I hit the panic button. We were going to have a baby! (Well, okay, LaVerne was going to have a baby—but I was on the team.) I wasn't ready!

I was too young. I was too inexperienced. I wanted to tell LaVerne, "Couldn't you just put it on hold for a few months until we are ready for this?" But that was not an option. It was time, and La-Verne gave birth to a beautiful baby girl. And somehow, by the grace of God, we learned that we were more ready to be parents than we had realized. Our own parents and friends were available for advice, and—amazingly enough—the baby did not break.

It is not easy to raise children, and most new parents feel unprepared when the first one comes along. Primed by racks of bestselling child-care manuals and how-to videos, parents are still uneasy about their ability to care for their child.

Just as many natural parents are unsure of their parenting skills, many potential spiritual parents feel insecure and uncertain. They simply do not feel ready! Yet one of the greatest catalysts for maturity as a Christian is becoming a spiritual father or mother. Parenthood challenges and even changes our perspectives. We overcome spiritual pride and are stretched in all directions of growth. This is how the Lord planned it so that we can grow in maturity in Christ. Even if prospective spiritual parents do not feel ready, as they take steps of faith and draw on the help and advice of their own spiritual moms and dads, they will find great success and fulfillment and discover that they are more ready than they had realized.

Yasuko came as a Japanese exchange student to attend a university near Harrisburg, Pennsylvania. Her host family, who served in a small group in our church, accepted her as one of the family and included her in all family activities, including a small-group Bible study that met in their community. Although her Buddhist parents had warned her to remain true to her upbringing, Yasuko was overwhelmed by the love and acceptance showered on her by these Christians.

Just two days before Christmas, her host family found her crying. When asked the reason for her tears, Yasuko explained, "I am so happy! I am going to give you a Christmas gift. I want to tell you that today I gave my life to Jesus!" Her host family and small group rejoiced! For the remaining few months Yasuko had in America, her host family became spiritual parents to her and helped her mature from a spiritual newborn to a spiritual young adult.

Yasuko returned to Japan and became a spiritual mother to many others as she continued to receive spiritual parenting via email from her spiritual mom and dad in Pennsylvania. She served as a youth leader in Japan and eventually went on to become a missionary to China, all while continuing to be mentored by her spiritual parents in America.

When parenting those who are spiritually parenting others, spiritual mothers and fathers should take several specific steps:

1. *Give their spiritual sons and daughters many opportunities to minister to and serve others.*
2. *Give honest, loving, constructive input to help the new spiritual parents grow in the faith and model Jesus more closely.*
3. *Try to work themselves out of a job.* Whatever role they presently have, spiritual parents should ask the Lord if He is calling those they mentor to take their places so that they can move on to something new the Lord may have for them.
4. *Open doors for their spiritual sons or daughters that will enhance their ministry as spiritual parents to others.* For example, provide them with opportunities to connect with new believers whom they can potentially mentor. Or perhaps you can suggest a book or a training course that will help them develop their skills as spiritual parents.
5. *Ask their spiritual daughters and sons for feedback and to describe their future plans.* Spiritual children need to be asked, "If you were me, what would you do differently?" and "What would you like to be doing five or ten years down the road?" Then the parents need to help them get there.

Although spiritual parents should be mature enough to give freely without thought of return, I think it is a good idea for spiritual daughters and sons to look for ways to bless their spiritual parents. Parents need encouragement, too! Occasionally they need to hear the actual words that describe how they are impacting the lives of those they are mentoring. Words and actions of blessing are powerful. Spiritual children can bless their spiritual parents by sending cards of appreciation, giving spontaneous gifts or telling them words of encouragement face-to-face.

I firmly believe the following biblical promise to natural children also applies to spiritual children: "'Honor your father and mother,' which is the first commandment with promise: 'that it may be well with you and you may live long on the earth'" (Eph. 6:2-3, *NKJV*).

As spiritual fathers and mothers encourage their spiritual children to grow up and have their own spiritual children, the relationship changes. Now spiritual parents talk to their spiritual children about their own parenting experiences. Spiritual fathers and mothers continue to parent their grown-up spiritual children as long as those children need the input; but in some ways, the children eventually become peers. But this relationship also may change: When children are babies, their parents meet all of their needs; when parents are elderly, the children often assume a role of responsibility for the wellbeing of the parents. Be aware of the possibilities of these potential changes in spiritual parenting relationships.

The Example of the Prodigal Son's Father

I was captivated by Henri J. M. Nouwen's description of his journey to spiritual fatherhood in his book *The Return of the Prodigal Son*. In the book, Nouwen—priest, professor and activist for social justice—tells of his fascination with Rembrandt's painting of the prodigal son in his father's arms with the elder son looking on (the three other people in the painting are nominal figures, barely discernible). Over the years since first seeing the painting on a poster, Nouwen agonized over whether he was the elder son or the prodigal in that picture. Then one day, a friend looked at him and spoke these powerful words:

> Whether you are the younger son or the elder son, you have to realize that you are called to become the father. . . . You have been looking for friends all your life; you have

been craving for affection as long as I've known you; you have been interested in thousands of things; you have been begging for attention, appreciation, and affirmation left and right. The time has come to claim your true vocation—to be a father who can welcome his children home without asking them any questions and without wanting anything from them in return.[2]

Like the father of the prodigal son, a spiritual father gives himself joyfully to his son because he loves him. Equipped with this affirmation and love, a son can claim his sonship and grow up and become a healthy father himself. Becoming mature requires selflessness, as Nouwen's friend pointed out. A selfless person gives people the opportunity to come through or fail while still loving them.

Whatever stage you are at in your spiritual growth and maturity, God's call on your life is eventually to become a mature spiritual parent, loving His children as He loves them—selflessly and without condition.

Key Questions for Practical Application

1. Fathers and mothers are role models to their growing children. In what specific ways can spiritual parenting be modeled to new believers?
2. Words are powerful in the lives of children. In what specific ways can you translate that effect into nurturing spiritual offspring?
3. In what specific ways do you love others selflessly?

for a Spiritual
Relationship

Part II

BECOMING A
SPIRITUAL MOTHER
OR FATHER

5

Looking for a Spiritual Parent Relationship

Key: If you do not have a spiritual parent, begin by becoming one.

There are three vital spiritual relationships that every healthy, growing person needs. The most common of these are what I call Barnabas relationships. These are the connections we have with our peers. Barnabas was the kind of person who saw beyond people's pasts and weaknesses and believed in their potential. He came alongside the new convert Paul and convinced the skeptical believers in Jerusalem that Paul was indeed a Christian and would no longer persecute them. While this connection began as a mentoring relationship, it later grew into a peer relationship when the Antioch church set them apart and sent them off as part of a team. They were peers who worked together on a missionary journey.

Just like Paul and Barnabas, we all need peers in our lives. Teenagers should have peer relationships with teenagers, parents with parents, doctors with doctors, pastors with pastors, and so forth.

The second relationship we need as spiritually maturing people is a Paul relationship. Spiritual daughters and sons have this kind of connection with their spiritual parents. Paul regularly referred to Timothy as his child or son[1] and also referred to some of his other converts in this way.[2] None of these young men were Paul's biological sons, but they all related to him as their spiritual father.

Third, there are Timothy relationships that are vital for every growing Christian to have. These are the connections spiritual parents have with the spiritual children whom they mentor and disciple, as we have explored.

It may seem ideal to begin with Barnabas and Paul relationships and then move on to Timothy-type relationships, but we cannot always build these connections in one particular order. Sometimes we must start where we are.

Peter and John had no formal education, but they spoke fluently to the scholarly religious leaders of the Sanhedrin: "When [the leaders] saw the courage of Peter and John and realized that they were unschooled, ordinary men, they were astonished and they took note that these men *had been with Jesus*" (Acts 4:13, emphasis added). A spiritual parent does not have to be a spiritual giant in order to train others. No one is a finished product. We are all learning to live in obedience to God and growing in grace. What really counts is our hearts and who resides there. The important thing is that we "[have] been with Jesus."

God takes common, ordinary people who love Jesus and transforms them by His presence. Spiritual growth is recognizing who God calls us to be and, through the power of the Holy Spirit, overcoming obstacles that stand in the way of maturity. God can use us to spiritually father or mother others at any point in our Christian walk—if we allow Him free rein in our lives.

As a young man, I worked on a construction crew building new houses. I learned that the first step to building a sturdy house is to put in a solid concrete foundation. It takes time to level the blocks and secure them with concrete, but a solid foundation keeps the house safe when the inevitable storms and winds come. This same principle is true of our spiritual lives. To become spiritual parents, we begin by building firm foundations on Jesus Christ. We get to know Jesus intimately and surrender to Him all that we are and hope to be. Only then can we be the safe and secure refuges He calls us to be for others.

When Is the Time Right?

Perhaps you are one of the many believers who have never had a spiritual father, a Paul relationship; this does not mean that you are unable to be one. If you feel you cannot become a spiritual parent until you have been parented yourself, break out of that small mindset! Instead, take a step of faith and see what the Lord will do. God's Word says you will reap what you sow (see Gal. 6:7). Sow whatever God has given you into another's life, and God will likely bring a spiritual parent into your life.

If you wait until you think you are ready to begin a Timothy connection with a younger believer, the connection will probably never happen. You don't need to be perfect, just faithful and obedient. Mother Teresa once said, "God does not demand that I be successful. God demands that I be faithful. When facing God, results are not important. Faithfulness is what is important."[3]

God knows both when we need a spiritual parent and when we are ready to become one. Abraham looked expectantly for a city designed and built by God, but he lived in a tent like a wanderer because the timing for God's promise was not yet right (see Heb. 11:8-10). Moses missed the timing of God when he killed an Egyptian, but God gave him another chance. The timing was finally right 40 years later when, at the burning bush, the Lord called Moses to lead his people out of bondage. Jesus worked in His earthly father's carpentry shop until the time appointed by the heavenly Father for Him to begin His public ministry. Later, Jesus infuriated the religious leaders of His day by His claims of deity; and they wanted to kill Him immediately, but "his *time had not yet come*" (John 7:30, emphasis added). Jesus continued to preach until the time appointed by the Father came for Him to go to Calvary (see John 13:1). God has the right time and the right relationships planned for us; we need only to seek His direction and obey.

Where Do I Begin?

The first place to begin a spiritual parenting relationship is in prayer. Start by praying that God will reveal the person you should parent. If you have tried to be a spiritual parent in the past and the relationship did not work out, continue to pray and trust God for His divine connections.

One of the most difficult aspects of a spiritual parenting relationship is finding the right person. Many times, the best relationships happen naturally: A conversation begins with another person, then a few more conversations take place, and soon you realize you have a spiritual daughter or son. There is no magic formula for initiating a relationship. You just have to go and do it. Every person is unique and will find what works for him or her. Although it is more common for the spiritual parent to initiate the relationship—this is the way Jesus approached His disciples—the initiation of a relationship can go either way. The spiritual mother or father may ask the spiritual daughter or son, or vice versa.

There should be a mutual attraction that draws the spiritual father or mother and the spiritual son or daughter together. If it is God's will, He will take that initial attraction and pull the relationship together in His timing. Your job in either role is to be the kind of person who is open, approachable and willing. Develop a reputation as a person who listens lovingly and attentively to others, and you will be surprised how naturally connections occur.

One approach to use when initiating a relationship is to identify things you have in common with a potential spiritual daughter or son—church, children, sports, hobbies or similar spiritual gifts. This person may be a friend, a coworker, a relative, a member of a small group you attend, a member of your local church or a person involved in ministry with you. Look for someone you feel comfortable working with and who will probably feel comfortable working with you, and then dare to make the first move!

Or perhaps you see someone who needs encouragement. Initiate a relationship by helping in practical ways. Babysit for a single mom so that she can have a night out. Go to the grocery store for a mother with toddlers. Spend time with a single person who seems lonely. Invite a younger person to watch a ball game or go to a movie, and write notes or make encouraging phone calls to that individual. Get to know his or her history. Share your testimonies with each other. Study a book together. Spend time together in

Bible study if he or she is a young Christian and needs to be grounded in the Word. Discover the areas of struggle the person has and pray for the person. If you are already a friend, you may feel God's tug at your heart to open your life more fully and transparently. Take a risk and be vulnerable. Make the time to invest in the relationship, and be strong on encouragement. As the relationship unfolds, you will experience the closeness of true spiritual friendship.

How Do I Know I'm on the Right Track?

Mutuality

The relationship, of course, must be mutual, because the purpose of any parenting relationship is mutual spiritual improvement and benefit. A key to successful spiritual parenting is when both the spiritual father or mother and the spiritual son or daughter desire to receive guidance and help. There must be a sense on both sides that there is reciprocal investment in the relationship. Both the spiritual parent and the spiritual child must recognize their need for the relationship. "Do two walk together unless they have agreed to do so?" (Amos 3:3). When there is mutual faith for the relationship, we are assured of its healthy existence, because faith is God ordained (see Eph. 2:8).

Both must want the relationship to work so that everyone can improve personally and spiritually, but the spiritual parent should seek to understand what the person he or she mentors desires to gain from the relationship. Then, with those expectations clearly understood, the spiritual parent can aim to fulfill their spiritual child's hopes by tapping into their own observations and experiences.

Love

It is essential for the spiritual parent and his or her spiritual child to enjoy and *like* being with one another. I like how Gunter Krallman describes how and why Jesus recruited His followers:

As a leader Jesus knew that the success or failure of his mission would decisively depend on the selection of the right helpers. Thus he took the initiative in calling men to become disciples, a step as unprecedented in rabbinic tradition as the fact that he called them to follow not just his teaching but him as a person. Jesus did not merely recruit them for their intellectual benefit or for a task, he recruited them for a relationship.[4]

In other words, in addition to training them, Jesus wanted *fellowship* with them. He loved them and enjoyed spending time with each one. He called the Twelve "that they might *be with Him*" (Mark 3:14, emphasis added). Love is the pivotal point on which a spiritual parenting relationship rests.

I find it interesting to note that though the word "disciple" is used over 20 times in the Gospels, Jesus Himself only used it 4 times (see Matt. 10:42; Luke 14:26-27,33). Jesus preferred instead to use the word "friend." More than wanting disciples or apprentices to train, Jesus wanted to have loving friend relationships with the spiritual sons He was mentoring. He knew that anyone can impress people from a distance, but you can only affect lives for eternity when you're up close and personal.

What If I've Tried and Failed?

A few years ago, Murray McCall, who has spent 10 years in church planting in New Zealand, told me, "After going through a season of discouragement as a spiritual leader, I came to understand that God had called me to be a father." This truth set him free as a leader in the Body of Christ. He realized that his primary call was to be a father, and he could trust God for grace to start again when he made mistakes or was discouraged.

The Bible is filled with models of impartation for us to imitate: from Moses to Joshua, from Elijah to Elisha, from Samuel to David, from Elizabeth to Mary, from Paul to Timothy and Titus. Regardless of disappointments or mistakes made along the way, every Christian must seek godly courage to become a spiritual father or mother and impart to others what God has given to him or her. It is possible and achievable, no matter what is in the past!

Dan Hitzhusen is a church planter who fondly recalls how his spiritual father, Josh McDowell, responded to his mistakes as a young leader:

> Josh saw me as a diamond in the rough. I was twenty-one years old with a heart for God, full of life, and full of myself. Serving as a personal assistant to Josh McDowell as a staff member of Campus Crusade for Christ, I made many mistakes. Josh expected excellence, yet, when I blew it, he would say something like, "Dan, that just shows it can happen to the best of them."
>
> I remember really messing something up and asking Josh why he didn't get particularly angry with me. He said, "Dan, the things that I think will make you a better person, a better friend, a better representative of Jesus Christ, I share with you. Everything else I take to God."
>
> On another occasion, I was feeling rejected by some of my co-workers. Josh pulled me aside and said, "Dan, you and I are renegades. We are different. We will never really fit in. You will never fit in. That isn't the way God made you."
>
> Josh always believed in me more than I believed in myself.
>
> Perhaps the greatest personal tribute that I have for Josh McDowell is that he saw me for who God made me to be and he encouraged me to serve God with my whole heart in my own uniqueness.[5]

Though Dan experienced disillusionment with himself and with others, his spiritual father never doubted that God had great plans for his life. No matter what you have experienced or perpetrated in the past, God has plans for your life, too.

Should I Wait?

After having experienced the lack of a spiritual father in my life for about 10 years, I made the decision to become a spiritual father to others. Amazingly enough, as I reached out to others who needed guidance and security and became a spiritual father to them, the Lord brought spiritual fathers into my own life.

I want to emphasize this: *Don't wait until you find a spiritual mother or father—become one yourself!* Waiting to acquire that wonderful spiritual mother or spiritual father who will perfectly nurture and love you before you reach out to parent others is like saying of your natural childhood, "My childhood was terrible. I grew up in a dysfunctional family. I'll never have kids, because I would be a terrible parent." This is simply not true! Each parent can begin with a clean slate. Parents, both natural and spiritual, can decide to learn from the past and make good choices along the way. If we wait until we receive all the spiritual nurturing we feel we need before we reach out to others, we will never fulfill the plan God has for each of us: growing into spiritual parenthood.

The Scriptures tell us to "cast your bread upon the waters, for after many days you will find it again" (Eccles. 11:1). Reaching out to parent another may look to you like throwing away your chance for having your own needs met, but when you sow into others' lives, God promises that you will reap a return.

I was teaching on spiritual parenting at a pastors' conference in Portland, Oregon, and an elderly man approached me between sessions to tell me a brief story about himself:

> I have been a spiritual father for many years. I was a staff member for Campus Crusade for Christ, and I was a spiritual father to students in the university. But I never had a spiritual father myself. Recently, however, I moved to Florida and began to attend a new church. A young man in church leadership approached me and asked me to go out for breakfast. After we ordered, he asked how I was doing and if I had any areas in my life that needed prayer. He wanted to pray for me on a regular basis. After our breakfast was over, he asked me to meet him again. And our breakfasts have continued since.

LARRY KREIDER

Then the elderly man looked at me with a twinkle in his eye. "Larry, I now have a spiritual father. He is twenty-nine years old!"

Relationships between the young and the old are a key to the Kingdom. The Lord wants to bring the young and the old together, bind them close to each other and to their God, and teach them to build His kingdom together. All it takes is willingness, availability, time and a generous dose of the grace of God. Open your hands and heart and look to Him for grace and direction.

Allow God to put together spiritual parenting relationships in His time. Become the spiritual mother or father He has called you to be and watch how He is able to bring exactly what you need. When you "cast your bread upon the waters," expect it to return!

Key Questions for Practical Application

1. Consider an occasion when you failed as a spiritual parent. How could you have handled the relationship differently?
2. Can you recall a time when a person much younger than you spoke a spiritual truth that challenged you?
3. Jesus fellowshipped with His disciples. In what specific ways do you make fellowship a vital part of spiritual parenting?

6

Finding Security in the Father's Love

Key: Only God can meet your need for a father's love.

Millions of people today believe that God is the Creator of the universe, but far fewer choose to know Him deeply enough to experience Him as their Father. Yet in His intercessory prayer, Jesus claimed that it is possible to know God in this way: "Now this is eternal life: that they may know you, the only true God, and Jesus Christ, whom you have sent" (John 17:3). God revealed Himself to us through Jesus Christ, and the entire gospel rests on this claim: Knowing God, through Jesus, brings abundant, eternal life. Our Father is a God of relationship. He wants to be our Father and have a personal friendship with us; and through that relationship, He wants to reveal His ways to us. When we know the Father and develop a love relationship with Him, we are secure as believers, willing and ready to reach out to others in love.

No earthly friendship, including the very best of spiritual mothering and fathering relationships, can substitute for this connection with the Father. Only the love of the Lord can impact our lives deeply enough to create lasting change, to transform our lives for eternity. Whether you are a spiritual father or mother or a spiritual son or daughter, you must keep your relationship with the Father primary, over and above all other relationships. As your friendship with God deepens, you will become increasingly freed and equipped to relate to others as a spiritual parent or a spiritual child, secure and grounded in the foundation of the Father's love.

Secure to Give Love Freely

Jesus knew He was a love gift from the Father to the world. He knew where He came from. He knew why He was here and where He was going. Because of this confidence, Jesus was secure in His calling and mission to freely and lovingly give of Himself without hesitation. As He guided and counseled His disciples and passed on the love that came from the Father, they in turn learned to give love freely, holding nothing back.

If we are to grow into healthy spiritual mothers and fathers, we must be confident of our Father's love for us and live in close relationship with Him. Only secure spiritual parents—those who are totally convinced that the heavenly Father loves them—can freely and lovingly pass on a healthy spiritual inheritance to the next generation.

And only spiritual children who are grounded in their heavenly Father's love can freely receive, take in and pass on the grace and wisdom they gain from their spiritual parents. Why do you think Jesus' disciples turned the world upside down in a few short years? They changed the world, not because they attended all the right seminars, but because they lived in close, intimate relationship with the right person and couldn't wait to freely pass on the overflowing abundance of God's love!

Gaining a State of Confidence

John, one of the 12 disciples of Jesus, became a father to the next generation of believers as he grew secure in the love of his heavenly Father. The Bible shows us that John and Jesus enjoyed an intimate, special friendship, as evidenced by identifying himself several times in his Gospel as "the disciple whom Jesus loved" (John 13:23; 19:26; 21:7,20; see also 19:26; 20:2). He even recorded that at the Passover supper, as was customary of the Greeks and Romans at mealtime, he reclined beside the Master, "leaning on Jesus' bosom" (John 13:23, *KJV*), an indication of close friendship and affection.

I think it's clear that John was totally convinced he was accepted and loved by Jesus! He knew Jesus like a brother and was a devoted friend. He was secure in the love of his Master. But how did John come to such a state of confidence and security in his life, enabling him to become a spiritual father and serve countless later followers of Jesus? It did not happen overnight.

Before John matured under the mentoring guidance of Jesus' loving influence, John's actions and attitudes were, to understate the matter, less than secure. He was hungry for status and power and seems to have had quite a few rough edges. John and his brother, James, were nicknamed the "Sons of Thunder" (Mark 3:17). I picture them as tough guys, perhaps the equivalent of modern inner-city gangsters, who secretly longed for security, belonging and identity. The brothers evidently had fiery tempers. When some Samaritans refused to allow Jesus and His disciples to come to their village, James and John asked Jesus if they could order fire down from heaven to burn up the inhospitable town (see Luke 9:54). At that point in his life, John certainly was not modeling the loving, giving Spirit of Christ!

John and his brother earned the anger of the other disciples when they asked a special favor of Jesus: "Let one of us sit at your right hand and the other at your left hand in glory" (Mark 10:37; see Mark 10:35-45 for the whole story). According to Matthew's version of the incident, the mother of John and James implored Jesus for the special favor (see Matt. 20:20-21). In either case, the brothers evidently struggled with issues of insecurity and self-aggrandizement. Another time, John saw a man driving out demons in Jesus' name, a man who was not a part of the "in" group. Because of his immaturity, John tried to stop the exorcist, and Jesus rebuked him for this attitude that caused him to exclude others who sought to follow Jesus (see Luke 9:49-50).

Later, however, we see that John imparted the Holy Spirit to Philip's converts in Samaria, the very people on whom he had wanted to call down fire for refusing to welcome Jesus (see Acts 8:14-16). It's obvious that something occurred in John's life in the intervening years. What happened? It was this: As John spent more time with Jesus, he was changed. Lengthy exposure to Jesus' extravagant love transformed the Son of Thunder into "the disciple whom Jesus loved."

In his Gospel, John recorded that Jesus told His disciples the secret of His love for them: "As the Father has loved me, so have I loved you" (John 15:9). How amazing! John received a revelation from Jesus that his Lord loved him just as much and in the same way as the Father loved His Son. This revelation opened the doors of John's heart so that he could give love freely to the next generation.

Even more amazing is that *we* are loved by the Father in the same way. When we become confident and secure in this knowledge, the doors of our hearts are opened, and we are able to love freely and without hesitation. It is not enough to experience God's perfect love—we must also be willing to give that love away, just as God did: "God so loved the world that he *gave*" (John 3:16, emphasis added). Giving love away helps us to live up to our full potential in God. It releases the joy of the Lord in our lives!

Giving Love Away

How do we give love away? By modeling God's love as we point our spiritual children to Jesus. In this way, love is multiplied through them. When our spiritual children see that we know the Father, they will want that same intimate, loving relationship for themselves. By observing our vibrant prayer lives—our very friendship with the Lord—they see that we are in love with Jesus. They will then want to experience firsthand the blessed knowledge that their heavenly Father loves them.

But spiritual children must be careful that they do not rely on the love of their spiritual parents more than they rely on the love of Jesus. Remember: Nothing can replace the heavenly Father's love in our lives.

Years ago, before I ever heard of the term "spiritual fathering," I discipled and spiritually fathered some young men who wanted to grow in their new Christian lives. Unfortunately, in my zeal I provided too much security for them, rather than allow them to discover how to place their total trust in Jesus. They began looking to me for that which only our Father in heaven could give them. My spiritual parenting relationship with each young man became an unhealthy bondage.

Looking to any leader for all the answers and putting him or her up on a spiritual pedestal is dangerous, because every leader is likely to fall off at one point or another! No wonder those I fathered spiritually became disillusioned and wounded. I did not have all the answers and I made mistakes; and because the young men were not grounded in the Father's love, my failures hurt them more than was necessary.

I learned a valuable lesson about the delicate balance of pointing people to the Father while fathering them to grow spiritually. We can parent and be parented effectively only if we rely completely on God's grace. Spiritual parents must constantly direct the gaze of their spiritual children toward Jesus, and spiritual children must strive to focus on their relationships with the heavenly Father before any other relationship. We can never have our emotional and spiritual needs met by the love of a spiritual parent. We must know our heavenly Father and experience His love and unconditional acceptance.

Charles Spurgeon once said, "The sheep are never so safe from the wolf as when they are near the shepherd." A close personal relationship with Jesus will keep spiritual children safe from harm, because their foundation, grounded in the Father's love, will be strong. And out of that security and confidence, they will, in turn, give love freely.

Secure to Serve Others

In the Upper Room during His last supper with His disciples, Jesus was so completely secure in the Father's love that He was able to serve His spiritual sons and expect nothing in return:

Jesus knew that the Father had put all things under his power, and that he had come from God and was returning to God; so he got up from the meal, took off his outer clothing, and wrapped a towel around his waist. After that, he poured water into a basin and began to wash his disciples' feet, drying them with the towel that was wrapped around him (John 13:3-5).

Grounded in Love

Mark, the author of the Gospel of Mark, was a spiritual son of the apostle Peter (see 1 Pet. 5:13) and didn't have the privilege of witnessing Jesus' sacrificial service to His disciples in the Upper Room. Whether or not Mark's shortcomings were due to not seeing Jesus firsthand, the evidence suggests that Mark had some problems accepting the heavenly Father's love. I believe it was this lack of solid grounding and confidence that resulted in a few problems when he was called on to serve. He deserted Paul on the apostle's first mission trip; and at the start of his second missionary journey, Paul refused to allow Mark to accompany him. This caused a rift between Barnabas and Paul, with Paul rejecting Mark and with Barnabas choosing to take the young man with him (see Acts 15:36-40).

Imagine being the unfortunate person responsible for splitting up the greatest church-planting team in history! In spite of Mark's shaky beginnings, however, Paul later forgave his wavering ways, telling the Colossian church to welcome him (see Col. 4:10) and then asking Mark to come and help him in his continuing ministry (see 2 Tim. 4:11).

I believe that somewhere along the way, Mark had a profound experience of his heavenly Father's love—this in addition to the persistent love of his spiritual fathers, Barnabas and Peter. It also must have helped that he had a praying mother; her house was a home to many praying people, including Peter (see Acts 12:12). Mark changed from a deserter to a faithful and useful servant of Christ, because he received a revelation that Jesus loved him unconditionally. The combination of a growing intimacy with the Father and the nurturing influence of spiritual parents on Mark's life caused him to grow up spiritually, ready to serve out of his grounding and confidence in God's love.

Molded for Service

When we become intimate with our heavenly Father and are willing to be influenced by faithful spiritual mothers and fathers, we too will be molded into the kind of people useful for service in God's kingdom. Knowing the Father transforms us and matures us into spiritual adulthood. Experiencing the reality of His love causes us to grow from spiritual babies to spiritual young women and men, and encourages us to take the next step and become spiritual parents.

The apostle John also learned how to serve humbly, following the example set by his Master. When Jesus asked him to prepare the Passover supper, he did so willingly (see Luke 22:8), and from this we can see the transformation love had already worked in his life. He no longer asked for special favors but instead was willing to serve. John had learned, by spending time with Jesus, that love knows no bounds and should be extended to all, even to those initially antagonistic to the Jews (for example, the Samaritans) or to the gospel. Getting to know Jesus intimately caused John to love as Jesus loved—fully and unconditionally, in service born from love.

John wrote the First, Second and Third Epistles of John, which are sometimes called the books of love because they are written from the heart of a loving father to his spiritual children. By the time they were written, John was thoroughly secure in his Father's love and longed to nurture and serve the scattered Church. Even later in life, when John was exiled to the isle of Patmos (where he wrote the book of Revelation), he continued to serve the growing Body of Christ from afar, confident and grounded in God's love for him. Jesus' love molded John into a revered and loved disciple who spent his life in service to the Father and His children.

Like John, we must be willing to serve the Lord in any way He asks. And when we know God loves us completely and unconditionally, we will be willing to do whatever He directs and to serve wherever He sends us.

Secure by God's Affirmation

During the early 1990s, I went through a season when I felt like a failure in ministry and leadership. Though I was serving as the pastor of a rapidly growing church, I wanted to quit. Even with all of the outward signs of success, I was tired and felt unappreciated and misunderstood. I secretly thought it would be better to leave church leadership behind and go back into the business world.

In the midst of my struggle, I stopped in to see Steve Prokopchak, our staff counselor. I asked him for his evaluation of the reasons I was not able to lead in a way that some on our team felt was appropriate and effective. Steve gently offered me some kind advice and then encouraged me to listen to a cassette tape he thought might be helpful (this was before the days of CD recordings and iPods).

In the car a few days later, I popped the cassette into my tape player to see what the speaker had to say. He immediately caught my attention as he talked about leaders who have a messiah complex, who feel that they need to have all the answers and be everyone's savior. I was glued to the speaker's words, because it almost seemed as if he was talking directly to my situation.

Then it dawned on me: *I* was the speaker on the tape! I rarely listen to recordings of myself and had not recognized my own voice. Then it all came back to me: I had taught a pastors' training course at our church the year before, and the recording captured my words to the future pastors, encouraging them to recognize the Lord as the only One who could ultimately meet their needs. A year later, I had not taken my own medicine, and I was paying for it!

On Steve's advice and with the affirmation of the leadership team of our church, I took a three-month sabbatical. It took me about five weeks just to feel human again; but during those months off, I began to deeply understand that significance and security cannot come from what I do or from what people think of me. In an undeniable and personal way, the Lord revealed that my value comes from His love for me. And God loves me just because He loves me, not because of what I do or what people think of me.

I keenly remember pacing back and forth in a cabin in the mountains, reading aloud from the Scriptures over and over again: "I have chosen you and have not rejected you. So do not fear, for I am with you; do not be dismayed, for I am your God. . . . For I am the LORD, your God, who takes hold of your right hand and says to you, Do not fear; I will help you" (Isa. 41:9-13). During a time of disillusionment and near burnout, I finally accepted that my significance comes from God's love for me—and that alone.

Although I had known this to be theologically correct for years, it had never sunk deeply into my spirit. The words of the song I had learned as a child took on fresh meaning: "Jesus loves me—this I know, for the Bible tells me so." I was changed! Whether or not people like me or affirm me is no longer an issue (of course it is still nice when they do), because I know in my spirit that God loves me!

I am whole because I personally experienced the Father's love in a real way. I do not need the affirmation of others, including my spiritual children; I have received the affirmation of my Father in heaven. Now I can be a spiritually and emotionally healthy spiritual father to others.

Robert McGee, a professional Christian counselor and lecturer, once said, "Who I think I should be is less than who I already am."

The transforming power of Jesus' love relationship with His disciple John demonstrates the singular importance of a close friendship with God. John loved and served his spiritual children without concerning himself with their affirmation or approval, because he was grounded in a confidence that came from knowing he was safe and secure in the love of the Father. We can love and serve out of that same confidence, whether as spiritual parents or spiritual children, and that ability to love and serve starts with us deeply knowing that "Jesus loves me—this I know, for the Bible tells me so." So simple, yet so powerful!

Key Questions for Practical Application

1. Are there situations that make you feel as if you have a messiah complex?
2. When was a time when insecurity forced you to recognize that God's love for you is more important than people's affirmations of you?
3. What are some pitfalls of spiritual parenting, and what are the solutions to overcoming them?

Healing the Past

Key: God can heal past wounds and restore His people for service.

If you or your potential spiritual daughter or son has been wounded in a past discipleship relationship, it is incredibly important for both your sakes that the wounded person seek healing. People with unhealed emotional and spiritual wounds have a strong tendency to inflict similar wounds on others, but their wounds *can* be healed.

Wounds from Past Spiritual Parenting Relationships

When There Has Been an Abuse of Authority
Abuse of power warps the blessing of spiritual mothering and fathering. Spiritual mothers and fathers are not to be dominating authority figures who coerce their spiritual children into submission. Instead, they are to tread lightly as they point their spiritual children to Jesus. I like how pastor Floyd McClung, in his book *The Father Heart of God,* describes the much-needed balance we need to exercise in the area of spiritual mentoring:

> Godly fathers want to serve others, and treat all men and women as their equals. Their actions proceed from an attitude of equality, not authority, because they are more concerned with serving than ruling.

Biblical authority is never taken; it is offered.... It comes
from the anointing of God's Spirit and is the sum total of
one's character, wisdom, spiritual gift, and servant attitude.
Fathers in the Lord understand these principles about
authority. They know the character of the Father, so they
are relaxed in their ministry to other people.... They have
learned to take action as God directs, and not just because
they are "the leader."[1]

Note below the differences between fathers who abuse their
authority and fathers who are in the Lord (these of course apply as
well to mothers):

Domineering Fathers
1. Function as if they alone are the source of guidance for
   people's lives.
2. Emphasize the rights of leaders.
3. Set leaders apart and give them special privileges.
4. Seek to control people's actions.
5. Emphasize the importance of the leaders ministering
   to others.
6. Use rules and laws to control people and force them to
   conform to a mold.

Fathers in the Lord
1. Believe that God is the source of guidance, and desire to
   help other Christians learn to hear His voice.
2. Emphasize the responsibilities of leaders.
3. Emphasize the Body of Christ serving one another.
4. Encourage people to be dependent on God.
5. Emphasize the importance of equipping the saints for
   the work of ministry.
6. Provide an atmosphere of trust and grace to encourage
   growth.[2]

Healthy spiritual parents earn the right to speak into their spiritual children's lives because they do so with the hearts of servants,

affirming and encouraging their children in their walks with Christ. A level of trust is built over time in balanced relationships that encourage those who are being mentored to be dependent on God.

If you are a spiritual parent or a spiritual child who is in a discipling relationship that is abusive, seek outside help now. Unhealthy relational ties can be very hard to discern when you are so close, and they can be even harder to disengage. Seek the counsel of your pastor or another church leader who is somewhat removed from the relationship. Be honest about what is taking place, allow the counselor to evaluate the dynamics of the relationship, and follow the suggested guidance for restoring the relationship or bringing it to a close. Above all, cover the situation in prayer.

Perhaps you feel hindered in the present by some of the experiences you had in the past. Maybe you were abused, hurt, disappointed, held back or lacked a healthy role model to follow. The Lord has a great plan for you. You can be restored!

The enemies of God's people ridiculed Nehemiah and his workers as they started to rebuild the wall around Jerusalem, the wall that had been broken down for ages and whose stones were charred and useless. The enemies mocked the Israelites: "What do these people think they can do with this mess? Can these burned stones live?" (see Neh. 4:2). They did not want to see Jerusalem become secure and safe again, because they wanted to continue running roughshod over its boundaries.

The devil is throwing similar accusations at God's people today: "How do those Christians expect to function with all the baggage from broken relationships with their parents? They've made too many mistakes. How can they expect to help someone else?" Perhaps you sincerely tried reaching out to another and the relationship deteriorated, so you feel like a failure. Maybe a spiritual father you looked up to used control and legalism to get his point across. Devastated and hurt, you tell yourself you will never place yourself in a position to be hurt again. These damaging thoughts come from the devil, who wants to rob you of hope and can keep you defeated and discouraged.

You must believe that although your own resources are few, you *can* be restored to carry out God's work. You can place your full trust in the overruling providence of God. The burned stones of Jerusalem's wall were charred and looked useless, but God's people chose not to look at their difficulties. Instead, they trusted the Lord. Because they concentrated on rebuilding the wall and refused to be discouraged, the scarred stones once again saw service in the wall around Jerusalem. The Israelites achieved their goal. And you can too.

When There Has Been Abandonment

Have you ever felt as if someone "dropped" you, crippling you for life? I meet so many people with a clear call of God on their lives but who feel as if they have been burned emotionally, or abandoned, by someone they had trusted. Some were burned by the deterioration of a relationship they had invested in and developed. In other cases, they were disillusioned when natural parents or spiritual parents disappointed them, and they gave up. These wounded people often live in deep disappointment and fear that they will never be loved and that the Lord will never be able to use them.

Not too many years ago, Cedric, who now leads a thriving family of churches in East Africa, felt burned, or abandoned, in such a way. He had worked side by side with a missionary, and the two had planted about 400 churches in Cedric's native country. He had looked to this man as a spiritual father, but the relationship began to unravel when Cedric started to notice that money was the bottom line for the missionary. It turned out that the missionary cared little about the souls brought to the Lord through church planting; he was motivated by financial gain. He hadn't loved his spiritual son as Cedric had believed—he had only used Cedric to enrich himself.

Cedric attempted to untangle himself from the missionary's web of deception and greed, narrowly escaping harm when the missionary sent thugs to burn Cedric's house down. Shell-shocked and grieving, reluctant to ever trust again, Cedric moved to a neighboring nation and enrolled in a university. While there, he fellowshipped at a church where people reached out in love to him. As he was restored, he took a step of faith to take up his mantle as a spiritual father. God began to use him as a leader in small-group ministry, and he later returned to his native country to plant a church.

Cedric was willing to start over because he refused to be intimidated by Satan's discouraging lies. A burned stone emotionally, Cedric did not give up, and he was healed! Today, he serves as a spiritual father to pastors all over his nation.

If Cedric's wounded heart and spirit can be restored, yours can be, too.

Foundational Beliefs for Restoration to Begin

Believe the Past Can Be Redeemed

In the first chapter of Matthew, we read the genealogy of Jesus. Why was this very long list of ancestors included in God's Word? Two reasons: (1) it demonstrates how people, specifically families, are important to God; and (2) it shows how a family can thrive and be blessed in the midst of the successes and failures of its individual members.

God wants each family to pass on a blessing to the next generation. The Bible is a book recorded for the generations as a record of the rich inheritance of relationships down through the generations. God honors and places importance on a family's lineage because each family has a unique story to tell. The people included in Jesus' genealogy had a part in seeing Jesus trained and fathered during His years on Earth. God the Father put Jesus on loan to Joseph and Mary so that they could train Him. Jesus' "foster father" trained Him in a carpentry shop. In order for Joseph to train Jesus, there had to be faithful individuals in his lineage who passed on a legacy of training. The life of Jesus was based on previous generations whose faithfulness had a direct bearing on His ministry.

In the same way, if we are to pass on an inheritance to others, we must receive a spiritual blessing from the generations past. We need healthy spiritual fathers and mothers to deposit a rich inheritance into spiritual sons and daughters.

Sometimes, however, previous generations feel more like skeletons in the closet than legacies of inheritance. Jesus' genealogy includes Rahab, a prostitute who delivered the wicked city of Jericho to the Israelites. The Lord redeemed Rahab's sinful past, and what was passed down through the generations was her obedience to God and compassion for the Israelites—not her shame. Her salvation is evidence that God redeems and restores future generations when even one individual turns to God in faith. Even an ungodly family member can be redeemed and the entire next generation turned to the Lord.

We must build on the shoulders of those who have gone before us, regardless of the mistakes they have made. We need to live in a posture of praise to the Lord for those who birthed us and nourished us both naturally and spiritually, and we must expect Him to redeem any shame in generations past. We also must purpose in our hearts that, by the grace of God, we will be positive influences on and give a good inheritance to the next generation.

Believe God, Not the Lies of the Enemy

We cannot believe the lies of the enemy and expect to live victoriously. If we justify our current negative situations by blaming them on past bad experiences, we will wallow in bitterness and unforgiveness. If we feel unable to fulfill the Lord's call on our lives because we have believed the lies of the enemy, we will be spiritually paralyzed and unable to fulfill our mandate as spiritual parents.

Mephibosheth, whose story is told in 2 Samuel, was a young man who lived the first part of his life believing a lie. He hid out in the town of Lo Debar, believing his life was in great danger. Because his grandfather Saul was no longer the king of Israel, he was told it was only a matter of time until David, the new king, found and killed him. He undoubtedly had been told stories about how typical it was for a new king to solidify his position by killing all family members of the former king.

Mephibosheth lived, not only in the emotional pain brought on by his fear of being killed, but in the physical pain he suffered as well. While still a small child, he had been crippled when a servant girl dropped him as they were fleeing from the new king's advance on the palace (see 2 Sam. 4:4). So he was emotionally and physically scarred—burned and broken, unable to fulfill his destiny.

One dreaded day, the new king's servants arrived in Lo Debar to find the grandson of King Saul. When they brought him to the palace, Mephibosheth fell on his face in terror and prostrated himself before King David, awaiting the death sentence he was certain he would hear. But then, Mephibosheth couldn't believe his ears: He heard the king say, "Don't be afraid, . . . for I will surely show you kindness for the sake of your father Jonathan. I will restore to you all the land that belonged to your grandfather Saul, and you will always eat bread at my table" (2 Sam. 9:7).

Unknown to Mephibosheth, David had made a covenant with Mephibosheth's father, Jonathan, years before. Each had pledged to take care of the other's family if anything ever happened to one of them. When Jonathan was killed in battle with his father, Saul, David remembered his covenant with his best friend. And he was committed to keeping his promise!

For years, Mephibosheth had believed a lie. He had been convinced that David would kill him, but all the while David was pursuing him with his best interests at heart. Mephibosheth was esteemed by David and given the honor of sitting at the king's table. Every need Mephibosheth had was completely met.

In the same way, our King longs to meet our needs for spiritual growth and deep relationships. If we believe the lies of the enemy instead of believing that God will guard our hearts and care for us, we may never allow ourselves to come out of hiding and be found in Him.

Believe the Lord Will Vindicate You

Perhaps you believe you have made a mistake from which you never will recover. Maybe you tried reaching out to someone and they exploited you in some way. Perhaps, like Cedric, a spiritual parent has hurt and taken advantage of you, or you feel misunderstood or falsely accused of a wrong.

God's Word cautions us away from trying to vindicate ourselves when others falsely accuse us of a wrongdoing (see Deut. 32:35-36; Rom. 8:33-34; 12:17-19). Instead, we should "drink the cup," and the Lord will vindicate us. According to Numbers 5:11-31, a man who suspected his wife of adultery was to bring her (and an offering) to the priest, who would have the accused woman drink dirty water from a cup. If she were guilty, she would get sick and diseased and become a curse among her people; but if she were innocent, the Lord would vindicate her, and she would be fruitful and bear children. Either way, she had to drink the cup!

God knows our hearts. He knows the truth. It does not help the situation to try to prove our innocence on our own; God has to do it. Certainly this does not mean that if someone makes a serious false accusation against us, we should ignore it and hope it will go away. We can respond in a spirit of humility and address the false accusation, but then we should lay it down and allow God to defend us. Our role needs to be one of forgiveness, or we will harbor resentment.

The Bible says there are two types of ministries before the throne of God—intercession and accusation: Jesus intercedes for us before the Father, but the devil accuses us before the throne (see Rom. 8:34; Rev. 12:10). The enemy can never triumph over the Son (see Rev. 17:14).

A former co-laborer in church leadership who left our church several years ago came back to meet with me and one of my colleagues a few years later. The Lord had spoken to him and challenged him concerning which of the two ministries before the throne of God he was embracing. To his surprise and regret, he had realized he had been participating in a ministry of accusation against me and against the Church. It had crippled him and robbed his joy. The Lord had convicted him of his judgmental spirit and he sincerely repented. Today, this precious man of God is one of our personal intercessors. The Lord vindicated me and redeemed our relationship!

If Satan uses someone to lie about us, though it may be tempting to lash out and try to vindicate ourselves, we must simply "drink the cup," acting with a spirit of humility and forgiveness and having faith that the Son will intercede. God is the vindicator.

Believe the Father Will Restore You
Spiritual mothers and fathers in the Body of Christ must grasp this simple, important truth: We need to forgive others just as we

want to be forgiven; we must extend mercy to each other and leave the judgment to God (see Luke 6:37). "Mercy [always] triumphs over judgment!" (see Jas. 2:13). Mercy entails letting someone off the hook because of love; it does not entail giving punishment or retribution that is deserved. When we extend mercy to those who have wronged us or made mistakes, those individuals can be restored and rebuilt.

The story is told of rebuilding the temple wall in Nehemiah 4. The enemies mocked those who were looking to God for help as they worked. They asked, "What are those feeble Jews doing? Will they restore their wall? Will they offer sacrifices? Will they finish in a day? Can they bring the stones back to life from those heaps of rubble—burned as they are?" (vv. 2-3).

In a similar way, Satan mocks the one struggling: "Can you, a burned stone, live and be of use?"

God gave Nehemiah a strategy to defeat the enemies, and the battle cry of the rebuilders became, "Our God will fight for us!" (Neh. 4:20). Today, we have Jesus, our intercessor, who is standing at the right hand of God interceding (fighting) for us (see Rom. 8:34). The promise in Romans 8:37 is that in everything "we are more than conquerors through him who loved us."

Failure does not mean God will not restore and use us again. Jesus answers loudly and clearly: "Yes, I will restore you and place you back on My wall for service in My kingdom."

We cannot look at our natural circumstances and give up. Our God is a God who forgives and restores people. Mercy illustrates what God is like. Our merciful Lord wants to restore those who have been wounded by abuses of authority or have been abandoned in some way. God's Word is clear in its encouragement to the downtrodden:

> And the God of all grace, who called you to his eternal glory in Christ, after you have suffered a little while, will himself restore you and make you strong, firm and stead-fast (1 Pet. 5:10).

> Though you have made me see troubles, many and bitter, you will restore my life again; from the depths of the earth you will again bring me up (Ps. 71:20).

For our light and momentary troubles are achieving for us an eternal glory that far outweighs them all (2 Cor. 4:17).

He wants us back in fellowship with Him and others. When we are wounded by others through spiritual abuse of authority or spiritual abandonment, we can feel like burned stones. Nevertheless, the Lord is redemptive! He heals burned stones and replaces them on the wall of service.

I know firsthand what this restoration is like. I felt like a burned stone for a period of time while I served as a pastor:

> During the spring of 1992, I was ready to quit. I felt misunderstood, and I wasn't sure if it was worth all the hassle. I told LaVerne one day, "If I get kicked in the head one more time (figuratively speaking), I don't know if I can get up again."
>
> As the senior leader [of our church], I was frustrated, exhausted, and overworked. God had given me a vision to be involved in building the underground church, but in the last few years we had strayed from that original vision. My immaturity as a leader, lack of training, and my own inability to communicate clearly the things that God was showing me led to frustration. In a misguided attempt to please everyone, I was listening to dozens of voices who seemed to be giving conflicting advice and direction. I felt unable to get back on track. I was tired and was encouraged to take a sabbatical.[3]

On that sabbatical, the Lord restored me and gave me new direction. I am grateful that He gave me the grace to continue and to believe again, because today I feel as if I have been made whole again—I have been replaced on His wall of service. Since that time, the Lord has placed spiritual fathers in my life to encourage me, and learning the incredible value of spiritual fathering has changed my life! It has become my life's mission to be obedient to God and train others to become spiritual parents. I am so blessed that the Lord would not allow me to quit—I am more fulfilled in serving God now than ever before.

I love the modern-day story of the restoration of a son to his father:

Sawat had disgraced his family and dishonored his father's name. He had come to Bangkok to escape the dullness of village life. . . . When he first arrived, he had visited a hotel unlike any he had ever seen. Every room had a window facing into the hallway, and in every room sat a girl. . . . That visit began Sawat's venture into Bangkok's world of prostitution. . . . Soon he was selling opium to customers and propositioning tourists in the hotels. He even went so low as to actually help buy and sell young girls, some of whom were only nine and ten years old. It was a nasty business, and he was one of the most important of the young "businessmen."

Then the bottom dropped out of his world: He hit a string of bad luck. . . . He finally ended up living in a shanty by the city trash pile. Sitting in his little shack, he thought about his family—especially his father, a simple Christian man from a small southern village near the Malaysian border. He remembered his dad's parting words: "I am waiting for you." He wondered whether his father would still be waiting for him after all that he had done to dishonor the family name. . . . Word of Sawat's lifestyle had long ago filtered back to the village.

Finally, he devised a plan. "Dear father," he wrote, "I want to come home, but I don't know if you will receive me after all that I have done. I have sinned greatly, father. Please forgive me. On Saturday night, I will be on the train that goes through our village. If you are still waiting for me, will you tie a piece of cloth on the po tree in front of our house? (Signed) Sawat. . . ."

As the train finally neared the village, he churned with anxiety. . . . Sitting opposite him was a kind stranger who noticed how nervous his fellow passenger had become. Finally Sawat could stand the pressure no longer. He blurted out his story in a torrent of words. As they entered the village, Sawat said, "Oh, sir, I cannot bear to look. Can you watch for me? What if my father will not receive me back?"

Sawat buried his face between his knees. "Do you see it, sir? It's the only house with a po tree."

"Young man, your father did not hang just one piece of cloth. Look! He has covered the whole tree with cloth!" Sawat could hardly believe his eyes. The branches were laden with tiny white squares. In the front yard his old father jumped up and down, joyously waving a piece of white cloth, then ran in halting steps beside the train. When it stopped at the little station, he threw his arms around his son, embracing him with tears of joy. "I've been waiting for you!" he exclaimed.

Sawat's story poignantly parallels Jesus' parable of the Prodigal Son, found in Luke 15:11-24. Christ told of another son who threw his life and money away in a whirlwind of wrong choices and fearfully returned home in the hopes that his father would take him back. He too was met with open arms and was loved and accepted unconditionally.[4]

Like the father in the story of the prodigal son, the Lord waits with open arms for all those who return to Him. He longs to restore us. His forgiveness and acceptance are always extended. We cannot allow Satan to deceive us; we must instead turn toward our loving Father who runs to meet us as we turn toward home.

Do you know that according to the Bible, Jesus Christ became a curse for us so that we could be set free from the devil's lies? "Christ redeemed us from the curse of the law by becoming a curse for us. The reason the Son of God appeared was to destroy the devil's work" (Gal. 3:13; 1 John 3:8). We can be free from the devil's lies because we are free from the curse. We do not have to live in bondage.

The Lord is a great Redeemer. He is waiting for us to stand up and be used, even if we have made mistakes. Do you know any natural parents who have never made any mistakes? Of course not! God gives grace to parents who place their faith and confidence in Him. God gives spiritual parents the same grace. As spiritual parents, we will probably make some mistakes, but the Lord will be there to cover the blunders we make. We cannot afford to stunt our spiritual growth and languish on the sidelines because of some mistaken belief that we cannot be used.

Steps to Take for Restoration

Perhaps you feel as if you have failed as a natural parent and that this disqualifies you from being an effective spiritual parent. Nothing could be farther from the truth! The Lord will use your disappointments and failures as a "sword in your hand" against the enemy. The Word of God is the sword of the Spirit (see Eph. 6:17), and a believer who learns how to maneuver the sword during times of disappointment will discover God's faithfulness, which empowers him to help others. That's what one man experienced when he battled deep depression after he lost his job. During those dark times, he cried out to God. He read Scriptures such as "never will I leave you; never will I forsake you" (Heb. 13:5), and by faith he chose to verbalize God's promise rather than the negative emotions that swirled within him. Just like Hebrews 4:12 tells us, the Word of God is a sharp sword. It broke the iron bands of negativity that had kept this man captive. Since then, because he learned to wield the sword of God's Word with skill and effectiveness, he has helped others who are struggling through dark times.

You will be the spiritual parent God has called you to be when you are grounded in a deep humility and trust in the grace and mercy of the Lord.

I have met many Christians who lacked a decent role model for fathering. Although they witnessed dysfunctional, faulty father images while growing up, they allowed the Lord to mold them into godly role models for their own children. They broke from their pasts. A negative parenting role model is no excuse for continuing to pass on bad parenting. God is "a father to the fatherless" (Ps. 68:5). He loves us and will teach us to be healthy parents. As we pour our lives into people and love them with the love of Jesus, we will model positive family patterns.

We live in a fallen world, but we were raised with Christ when we were redeemed, bought back by the blood Jesus shed on the cross 2,000 years ago. Jesus came to set us free and to give us abundant life (see John 8:32; 10:10). Step by step, we reclaim what Satan has stolen from us—in our homes, in our workplaces, at school and in the rest of the world around us. God has a loving plan of redemption for every believer and seeks to accomplish His plan by restoring ordinary people like us.

If you are one of those who have been abused or abandoned—burned or broken—take a step of faith, trusting the Lord to restore your wounded heart: He will heal you completely and place you back on the wall of service.

Are you ready to believe? If so, begin by taking the five steps for restoration:

1. *Unlock the door.* If you hide behind a locked door, attempting to bulletproof yourself from hurts, you will actually end up hardening your heart. God wants to expose and free you. How? It's simple. Jesus said that when you believe in Him, you "will know the truth, and the truth will make you free" (John 8:32). Jesus Christ, who is "the truth," makes you free (John 14:6)! You become free from being a captive to sin—to your hurts, mistakes, prejudices and false notions that entangle and enslave your soul. Through faith, unlock the door of your hardened heart and fall into the arms of Jesus, whose "yoke is easy" and whose "burden is light" (Matt. 11:30). Trust Jesus to restore your life.

2. *Stake your claim.* God promised the children of Israel the fertile land of Canaan. It was their land because God promised it to them, but they had to receive it by going in, taking it from their enemies and staking the claim for themselves. The same truth applies to you. You stake your claim on a restored and abundant life by taking back the areas of your life that the devil has

stolen from you. If the devil has stolen your peace, your joy, your health or your hope, today is your day to claim it back from the enemy! Claim back from the devil the specific areas he has stolen from you. When you take Christ at His Word, the Lord honors His covenant with you!

3. *Receive prayer from a trusted friend.* For help in your restoration process, seek the counsel of a godly friend or spiritual parent. He or she can walk with you as you ask God's forgiveness, receive healing for your wounded emotions and gain the strength to "sin no more" (John 8:11, *KJV*). James 5:16 tells us, "Therefore confess your sins [faults] to each other and pray for each other so that you may be healed. The earnest prayer of a righteous person has great power and wonderful results."

4. *Be patient.* The process of restoration may not happen overnight. Corrie ten Boom, who experienced life in a Nazi concentration camp, attested to the bell theory when it came to finding complete healing. She said that when you ask the Lord to heal and restore you, the devil will try to bring the old emotions of hurt and pain back to you again and again. But like the clanging sound of a church bell that rings loud at first and then grows softer and softer until it finally stops ringing, the hurts will grow fainter and more distant as you forgive others and continue to daily claim healing and restoration for your life.

5. *Keep growing.* God is calling you to be a healthy, functional spiritual parent. Even if you have not had a spiritual parent yourself, the Lord will teach you to be a spiritual mother or father to the next generation, if you keep your eyes on Jesus. Joseph, a man of moral and spiritual strength, was likened to a fruit tree with branches going over the well wall (see Gen. 49:22). The moisture from the well kept the tree watered and bearing fruit. Like Joseph's branches, your branches will grow abundantly over the wall when you are constantly watered by the Word of God and the Holy Spirit and focus on reaching

out beyond yourself. You will bear fruit for Him in the form of many spiritual children.

Our God is restoring spiritual fathers and mothers to their sons and daughters and gently placing them back on His wall of service. God is calling forth His people who have been burned and broken in these days, and He is healing them and giving them jobs to do.

You must find your place on the wall. God loves to use burned stones! If you are a burned stone, receive the grace of God today from your heavenly Father and be made whole through His Son, Jesus Christ. God wants to bless you, make you strong and give you a great inheritance of spiritual children.

Key Questions for Practical Application

1. Have you ever felt wounded by a spiritual relationship? If so, what are the steps you believe you should take to find healing?
2. What are some lies the enemy has used to keep you from living victoriously? How can your past be redeemed?
3. How has God's unconditional love impacted your life?

Expanding the Number of Spiritual Parents

Key: Multiple spiritual parents produce multiple spiritual parents.

Many times God uses more than one spiritual mother or father in a person's life to meet various areas of need. For example, a spiritual parent may counsel someone specifically in the area of healthy family relationships, while another spiritual parent may offer expert tips on financial planning and budgeting. Yet another spiritual parent may mentor the same spiritual son or daughter in a specific area of Christian ministry. (For years, my natural father has served to teach me principles of sound financial management.)

Even ministry leaders need spiritual moms and dads. In spiritual fathering and mothering, the buck does not stop at any point in the family hierarchy! A pastor's wife may be mentored by another spiritually mature woman—preferably another pastor's wife who understands the needs of someone in the limelight. The senior pastor of a church needs a spiritual father, too—preferably one who might mentor him in sound decision-making and leadership principles. I have various spiritual fathers to whom I look for spiritual advice and continuing leadership development. Some are theologians, while others have a keen understanding of cross-cultural leadership. I need these fathers in my life if I hope to continue to grow and mature in Christ. I will never outgrow the need for a spiritual father.

Another kind of spiritual mother or father may be someone you have not met personally. For example, you may be tutored by individuals through reading their books or listening to their CDs, DVDs or podcasts; they mentor through their writings and teachings. One of the reasons I began to write over 20 years ago was that I had been so encouraged by others who had gone before me and written about what they had learned and experienced. I realized that I might help others in the same way others had helped me. Today, more than 30 books later, I continue to write about the spiritual truths I have learned through the "school of the Holy Spirit." I pass on to you what I have learned from others and from the Lord.

Types of Spiritual Parents

There are many types of spiritual parents who mentor their spiritual sons and daughters in a wide variety of arenas. Nelson Martin, a pastor who serves the DOVE International family by heading up a 24-Hour Prayer Watch for our family of churches, is a spiritual father to prayer leaders around the world. The prayer watch includes prayer generals who oversee prayer warriors who pray for the DOVE International family around the clock. Some of these prayer generals guide the prayer warriors under their care by teaching them to pray and hear from God, connecting with them in a prayer mentoring relationship.

Couples can play a vital role in parenting other couples in their marriage relationships. We have seen gratifying results in the DOVE International family of churches with a successful couple-to-couple marriage mentoring program. The workbook *Called Together*, written by Steve and Mary Prokopchak, is a unique mentoring program designed for use by mature couples who counsel and equip engaged couples for marriage and beyond.[1]

Young mothers need older mothers to help them become the wise, capable parents God designed them to be. Experienced business leaders can disciple younger business professionals in sound practices and ethics and help them achieve success. Someone who has lost his or her spouse years ago may counsel more-recent widowers and widows through their grief and adjustments. Seasoned missionaries can mentor developing missionaries. These "like" (or homogenous) kinds of spiritual parenting relationships can be incredibly beneficial.

My friend Earl is a successful businessman in our local community. He has told me that the most fulfilling activity in which he participates is meeting with younger business leaders and mentoring them through the potential pitfalls of business and life. He is a spiritual father in the marketplace.

I was thinking about going back into business a few years ago, possibly working on the side as I continued to write and teach in the nations. I have friends involved in ministry leadership who are also involved in business, and it works well for them. To evaluate the pros and cons of such a venture, I sat down with two of my business-leader friends and gave them my proposal. After talking with me and seeking the Lord's direction, they both encouraged me not to do it during this season of my life. They felt strongly that with my present schedule, adding something else to my life would not work. I took their advice and abandoned the potential business venture. I knew that the timing of God is critical, and today, I know I am better for having maintained my focus during that season on leadership in the Body of Christ. It pays to have spiritual parents in the marketplace. Today I am involved in another business with my son, Josh, which has been extremely fulfilling for me.

A few years ago I was seated next to a businessman on a flight to Seattle. We struck up a conversation and he asked me what I do for a living. I told him that I'm involved in Christian leadership training and that I write and teach on mentoring. He, in turn, told me that he is in a management role in one of the major airplane manufacturing corporations in America. Then he shared an amazing concept. He told me that his corporation had recently come to the realization that they had lost an entire generation's worth of brain trust in their company. They had neglected to mentor younger workers to understand the strategic plan and vision for the company. When the leadership realized the near-catastrophic mistake, they immediately decided that no one in management would advance in the company until they were actively engaged in mentoring the next generation.

Sometimes corporations use biblical truths to run their businesses, while we in the church continue to live by our misguided religious traditions. But this is changing. God is restoring the biblical truth of spiritual mothering and fathering to His people, and in some places He is using the corporate world to do it.

The Lord wants to use mature, knowledgeable believers—whatever their areas of expertise—to grow you into a thriving follower of Jesus, and He wants to use *your* passion and know-how to parent the next generation.

Multiplication of Parents

When our youngest daughter, Leticia, was in her senior year of high school, her school offered a program that allowed students to explore career possibilities by accompanying someone as he or she went through a normal day in the workplace. As the students followed the nurses, journalists, bankers, scientists, engineers, technicians and administrative professionals who served as their mentors, they got a professional's-eye look at that job and its workplace environment. Although the students were provided with information about various career paths, resources and programs, the school had found that shadowing—exposing students to different professions through up-close and personal contact—was the most valuable way to jump-start students' thinking about the limitless possibilities for their futures.

Similarly, by shadowing a spiritual mother or father in her or his daily life, a spiritual daughter or son learns the basics of spiritual parenting naturally, quickly and easily. Up-close and personal contact is the start of a powerful legacy—and the possibilities are limitless. (Though we must remember that legacies come after the fact. If we dwell on the end results, we may find ourselves easily overwhelmed.)

Spiritual parenting is a process, and sometimes it's a long one! But as each one parents someone else, the parenting efforts are multiplied. The unique teaching methods of Dr. Frank Laubach can give us a glimpse of just how greatly they can be multiplied:

> Dr. Frank Laubach's epitaph ascribes to him the fol-
> lowing title: "The man who taught the world to read."
> Dr. Laubach popularized the phrase "each one teach
> one." Via his simple four-word strategy of teaching one
> person to read under the condition that each would
> teach another to read, several million people have now
> experienced the thrill and freedom of reading for the
> first time. The chain continues to this day, long after his
> death. Today the Laubach method has more than eighty
> thousand volunteers worldwide.
>
> Pause for sixty seconds and try to imagine the
> implications of this: You mentor 12, who mentor 12,
> equaling 144!
> who mentor 12, equaling 1,728!
> who mentor 12, equaling 20,736!
> who mentor 12, equaling 248,832!
> who mentor 12, equaling 2,985,984!
> Is an unbroken chain of spiritual fathers and moth-
> ers realistic? Probably not! But the point is clear. Even
> if only a small fraction of spiritual sons and daughters
> follow through by mentoring someone else, a significant
> difference will be made in the number of leaders in the
> next centuries—or until the Lord returns![2]

It's obvious that the multiplication potential of spiritual parenting is phenomenal! Quite naturally, in spiritual family relationships, spiritual babies grow into young men or women and finally become spiritual fathers or mothers. And before you know it, a spiritual legacy is created. The explosive result demonstrated above is the natural multiplication that happens when each successive generation takes up the mantle of spiritual parenting. But the process multiplies with exponential force only when each generation refuses to wait until they are spiritual giants before they become spiritual parents. Each member of a generation must realize that she or he can *have* a spiritual parent and *be* a spiritual parent simultaneously (and in fact, that's how the process works best!). As each new generation steps up to the plate, spiritual fathers and mothers are constantly multiplied and released.

Key Questions for Practical Application

1. How has reading books and working with others influenced you to grow spiritually?
2. Contemplate the multiplication potential in the Laubach method ("each one teach one"). Write down the names of those whom you have influenced and the names of your potential spiritual children.
3. What are the benefits of having a spiritual parent while simultaneously being a spiritual parent?

Part III

PRACTICAL
INSIGHTS FOR
SPIRITUAL
MOTHERS AND
FATHERS

9

Copying the Jesus Model

Key: You need to initiate and build a relationship and then release your spiritual daughter or son.

When I was a young leader, I felt I needed to be everyone's friend on an equal basis. As you might expect, I soon found there was not enough of me to go around! As I prayed and pondered Jesus' relationships with His disciples, it became clear to me that Jesus worked within the same constraints we are bound by: He could effectively be in close spiritual fathering relationships with only a small number of people. The level of His relational investment did not depend on how long He had known His followers or on their expectations; He clearly heard from His heavenly Father regarding the disciples He should spend the most time with. Jesus did that which His Father led Him to do (see John 5:19); and thereby He gave us the perfect spiritual fathering model: Value all people, but develop deep friendships with only a few.

God created us to need others and to be needed by them. Jesus was God but also fully human, and He had the same relational needs we have. A spiritual parent will have relationships of varying levels of friendship and intimacy, and to sort these out, it helps to understand the sphere of relationships Jesus modeled and to apply these to spiritual parenting.

Jesus' Sphere of Relationships

Jesus had an inner circle of friends: Peter, James and John. He spent much quality time with these three, especially John. Beyond this

tight-knit circle, Jesus closely fathered the 12 disciples, with whom
He traveled day to day. Beyond those friendships, He was in relationship with the 72 disciples He sent out "two by two ahead
of him to every town and place where he was about to go" (Luke
10:1). Lastly, Jesus was a spiritual father to the 120 faithful believers who waited in the Upper Room for the promised Holy Spirit
(see Acts 1:15). Jesus also ministered to the multitudes, but this
was most often done in the company of and with the assistance
of His friends and disciples.

Jesus knew that Kingdom values are caught more than
taught, so He *initiated* close relationships with followers who
were ready to catch, and He spent the majority of His time *building*—nurturing and preparing—the Twelve to fulfill the Lord's
purposes for their lives. And when they were ready (and probably
before they *felt* ready!), He *released* them to live out the Kingdom
values they had caught and to continue His mission of initiating,
building and releasing even more disciples, who would, in turn,
all do the same. From the Sermon on the Mount to the Sea of
Galilee, from the Temple gates to the Garden of Gethsemane,
day in and day out, Jesus modeled healthy and effective spiritual
fathering. He fished, prayed, wept and rejoiced with the disciples
until they could follow His example and spiritually father many
more people in the kingdom of God.

When Jesus trained His disciples, He didn't do it sitting on a
hill somewhere, lecturing them for three years. He taught them
through real-life experiences as they traveled from place to place.
They actively learned, by Jesus' example and demonstration, how
to be a part of the kingdom of God. The disciples witnessed
God's power and compassion firsthand when they came to Jesus
with a very small amount of bread that He multiplied to feed a
huge hungry crowd. They learned to discern the true from the
false when Jesus exposed the scribes and Pharisees in their false
piety and self-righteousness and affirmed the true generosity
of the widow with two coins. Their fingers learned to heal the
sick, to give sight to the blind and to bring the lame to their feet
by watching the caring Master touch those who needed God's
healing. Their hearts were trained to love the oppressed, the poor

and the little children when they saw the heart of Jesus moved to show His care of them again and again.

After three years, the disciples were not perfect, but Jesus believed in them enough to entrust the Church to their care when the time came for Him to return to the Father. He knew they had caught the heart of the kingdom of God.

The Basics of the Jesus Model

At its most basic, the task of a spiritual parent is to follow the Jesus model of *initiating*, *building* and *releasing*. Spiritual parents invite their spiritual children into relationship (*initiate*), nurture and guide them (*build*), and *release* them to parent others.

Initiate

Jesus *initiated* His close relationships, choosing from 72 of His followers 12 friends to be His key disciples. He had known them, walked with them and watched their lives; but now it was time to get serious, so He prayed all night and chose the Twelve (see Luke 6:12-13). In the same way, those whom the Lord may call you to spiritually parent in a closer relationship will probably be those with whom you already have some type of friendship.

Taking your cue from Jesus, you as the spiritual parent must take the *initiative* and get to know your spiritual child well. To do so, you need to spend time with her or him, because getting to know someone takes intentional effort! You can start by spending time doing together something you both enjoy—fishing, scrapbooking, going to a sports game, baking cookies. You might talk about where you came from, your thoughts about your current status, and your hopes and dreams for the future. And be sure to ask them questions that apply to their lives about these same topics.

Build

After a solid foundation of relationship is laid, it's time to *build*. The goal of spiritual parents must be to equip and invest in their children to increase their effectiveness for the Kingdom, but this can take many different shapes.

If you are parenting someone for ministry, take that person along with you when you visit a sick member from your small group, or participate with the one you are mentoring in an evangelism outreach in your community. Let him or her see you serve by using your gifts and knowledge, and help your child grow in these areas, too.

If you are discipling a parent, invite her or him to spend time with you and your children. Let him or her watch as you discipline and shepherd your natural children, or tell your spiritual son or daughter stories about raising your kids. Be honest about your mistakes and challenges, your high points and low moments. Pray with your spiritual daughter or son when she or he struggles.

If you are parenting a student, be available to help with school work and to answer questions when ideas that seem to contradict God's Word are encountered. Whatever the particular situation, nurture and encourage your spiritual son or daughter to draw closer to the Father, to increase in knowledge and wisdom, and to spread his or her wings in boldness.

Release

Over the course of time, as you remain sensitive to God's leading, you will know when it is time to *release* your spiritual daughter or son into the next stage: parenting her or his own spiritual children. After a time of watching Jesus minister to others, the disciples were released by Jesus to do the same thing.

Many discipleship systems today are stagnant and limited and don't actually produce disciples. A pastor is paid to "feed the flock," and the people get their money's worth in good sermons and great programs. Too often, though, because the pastor is one person doing the work of everyone, the pastor burns out and moves on to another church; and the people never fulfill their calling in Christ to become equipped and empowered by His Spirit and then released as disciple-ministers themselves. They never become spiritual parents. We must change our focus on programs and our spectator mentality to a focus on empowering and parenting people in spiritual family settings and we must have a multiplication mentality.

If we don't change our focus and mentality and begin to release new generations of spiritual parents, the Church will continue to overflow with "emotional and spiritual orphans," according to Floyd McClung:

> So many people are orphaned, not just from their physical parents, but from any kind of healthy spiritual or emotional heritage. . . . The church is also filled with spiritual orphans. Either they have accepted Jesus Christ but have not been nurtured in their faith, or because of some failure on their own or someone else's part they have not yet become a part of a spiritual family. . . .
>
> These people desperately need pastoral care. They need to be taught God's Word, to be counseled with sound biblical principles, and to be encouraged and exhorted by someone mature in the faith. They need a spiritual father or mother who can help them grow in the Lord.
>
> Others need to be "reparented"—that is, given the kind of example that only a wise, stable mother or father figure can provide. If proper parenting was missing during a person's developmental years, whether physically or spiritually or both, he or she needs someone to provide an example. . . .
>
> Being a father or mother in the Lord is not limited to those who are pastors or spiritual leaders. There is also a very crucial need for other spiritually mature, caring people to act as "fathers" and "mothers" to other believers. . . .
>
> By their very presence, they minister to those around them because of their maturity and depth in God. We need to turn loose these "moms and dads" in the church to be who they are. By being available, having time for people, and having open homes, their lives can be instruments of healing and love.[1]

When you sense your spiritual child is ready, start on-the-job training! Ask for his or her input in a variety of situations. Find out what the person you are mentoring would do differently if your roles were reversed. Invite him or her to share any observations about your relationship and how it has progressed. Then determine how you can turn the observations into life or ministry principles.

As you observe your spiritual son or daughter testing what he or she has learned, it is important to do an evaluation and give feedback, including areas for suggested growth and improvement. This give-and-take allows the person you are mentoring to apply and adapt to her or his own situation what she or he has seen you do.

Listen attentively and respectfully as your spiritual son or daughter tells you about the "new" successful idea you have used a dozen times. Help the person you are mentoring analyze the causes if the idea fails or the reasons if the idea succeeds. Mistakes will be made—you can count on it!—but fledgling spiritual parents need to make their own mistakes and learn to deal with the consequences. Remember: Our God is a God of second chances. If Jonah could receive a second chance, so can you and so can your spiritual daughter or son! Encourage him or her to press on. Share your feelings, including feelings of fear and inadequacy. Be honest and vulnerable, and your spiritual child will learn to do the same for the next generation.

Give assignments to your spiritual daughter or son when it's clear from your conversations and observations that she or he is ready. If you are going to pray for a sick person, for instance, invite your spiritual daughter or son to tag along. Then the next time there is a need for prayer, ask your spiritual child to lead while you stay in the background, ready to lend support. Start with small things and increase to greater responsibilities. Eventually the person you are mentoring will be accompanied in prayer by her or his own spiritual children.

Get the picture? That's how spiritual children are released.

Other Facets of the Jesus Model

Build Relationships
In the Old Testament, God's people consisted of 12 tribes and a multitude of clans and families known corporately as the children of Israel. Through these family relational connections,

God demonstrated the importance of generational inheritance, which is passed from father to son. Receiving this inheritance, which was first promised to Abraham and then passed on to his descendants, depended on the flow of blessing from generation to generation.

In a similar fashion, Jesus counseled His disciples to grow His Church, based on parenting believers in spiritual families. The Early Church knew the importance of relational connections. The Scriptures tell us that God's people gathered at the Temple and met in small groups to minister to each other:

> So continuing daily with one accord in the temple, and breaking bread from house to house, they ate their food with gladness and simplicity of heart, praising God and having favor with all the people. And the Lord added to the church daily those who were being saved (Acts 2:46-47, *NKJV*).

The Early Church followed the disciples' example of spiritual parenting by meeting "house to house" to experience spiritual family life to its fullest. These assemblies were vibrant and alive. The believers had a deep love for each other, and joyfulness and generosity were the outstanding hallmarks of their relationships. They sold their possessions to provide for the needs of others. They remained steadfast in the apostles' teachings, learned to pray with results, rejoiced when persecuted and were willing to die for their faith. They were held in high honor by others who observed their lifestyle.

Relationships were the key to the explosive growth of the kingdom of God in the Early Church. In the house fellowship groups, spiritual families were raised and multiplied. Through small groups meeting in homes, members were nurtured, equipped to serve and could easily use their spiritual gifts to build each other up to become like Christ. They met together with joy and love for each other, and new people were continually added to the Church family. Who wouldn't want the vibrant connections these believers exemplified?

This kind of New Testament Church life, in which people were in relationship with each other and their God, is a model that today's spiritual parents must imitate. Healthy families have parents who take their God-given responsibility as fathers and mothers very seriously. John the apostle challenged the early believers to "practice loving each other, for love comes from God and those who are loving and kind show that they are children of God, and that they are getting to know him better" (1 John 4:7, *TLB*). Living in close relationships with others, which was ordained by God for the children of Israel and then replicated in the close friendships of Jesus with His disciples and their parenting of the next generations, reflects our understanding of God's design and intention for His people.

This small-group, family-like model is today springing up in all types of churches in nearly every nation of the world. Not too long ago I was in Brazil, where I spent time with a pastor friend who recently started a new church. Eight years after he began, there are more than 21,000 people in the church, all involved in small groups in which each one is parented by a spiritual mother or father. God is calling His Church back to the simplicity of spiritual family life, and the Church is growing just as it did in its earliest days.

The Bible says that we are living stones for God's use in building His house: "You also, as living stones, are being built up a spiritual house" (1 Pet. 2:5, *NKJV*). We, as redeemed people in whom God now resides, are living stones. We are built together with the mortar of God-ordained relationships into a spiritual house. Without these strong connections, we soon fall apart and lay as useless rubble on the ground.

Sadly, today there are many living stones lying useless on the ground. Many Christians, instead of being cemented to other believers in family-type relationships, are haphazardly thrown on a heap as they assemble once a week to hear a sermon, sing some songs and then leave without having had any real, bonding interaction. Instead of being the family God has called them to be, they come together every Sunday morning in a large gathering of relative strangers. Rather than experiencing the day-to-day love of a truly spiritual family, they experience a weekly family reunion.

There's a huge difference between the vibrant daily life of an immediate family and an extended family getting together for a weekly reunion. When long-lost relatives come together for a reunion, each person presents his or her best face to the larger family; and family members don't see each other often enough to know anything besides what they're told. They swap stories and testimonies about their accomplishments and extol their successes, like the fantastic goal Jeremy scored on the soccer team and Meagan becoming an honor student. But much of this hoopla, while worth celebrating, is superficial.

Members of an immediate family know, not only the accomplishments of the family members, but also their struggles, because they are there day after day. They know that Jeremy's low grades may result in him being eliminated from the team. They know that Meagan had to overcome a learning disability and apply herself to diligent study in order to attain the distinction of becoming an honor student, and they know that she suffers anxiety attacks. Immediate family members know each other inside out. They see the good, the bad and the ugly; and they still love each other and work as a unit to encourage each member. We too can be in an immediate family by being in close relationships with others in a small group of believers. The leaders of the small group are simply spiritual mothers and fathers to the group. We are already included in God's universal family because we are members of the Body of Christ, but we also need to experience personal spiritual family relationships.

Like an immediate family, a spiritual family readily shares both its struggles and its triumphs; the family members have transparent relationships, with spiritual parents to guide and nurture their spiritual children.

A few years ago in the Pacific Northwest, I met Sam, an airline pilot, and his wife, Janice. Sam grew up with a religious background but had been turned off by church. When his neighbor, Duane, invited him to attend a small-group meeting in his home, Sam at first declined. He wanted nothing to do with Christianity. The Christians he knew were self-righteous hypocrites, consumed with making sure others followed all the rules and regulations.

But Duane and the guys from the group persisted in connecting with Sam. When they saw that he was adding a room to his house, they offered to help. Sometime between hammering nails and laying down carpet, Sam's perception of Christians began to change for the better. These guys were real. They didn't spout a lot of overdone Christian clichés. They admitted their weaknesses and clearly "walked their talk."

Eventually Sam and Janice both gave their lives to the Lord, and the men and women in the small group next door became their spiritual fathers and mothers. As Sam gave up his bad habits one at a time, the men never condemned him but supported him as a family would. Today, Sam and Janice parent their own spiritual family of growing believers.

Duane as a spiritual father—and the guys in his small group—understood the importance of building relationships and making connections. They followed the example set by Jesus, and the family of God continues to grow.

See Potential

Recognizing the undeveloped traits, gifts and abilities of a spiritual daughter or son is a spiritual parent's responsibility. Jesus modeled this as well. He changed Simon's name to Peter, which means "rock." Peter didn't act like a solid, stable foundation stone when he fell asleep in the Garden or denied Jesus three times, but the Lord knew Peter's heart and saw his potential. The apostle later grew into the rock Jesus predicted he would become, and Peter encouraged his spiritual children, as we have seen, to become living stones in the same way.

Although a spiritual parent cannot predict the future of a spiritual child, the parent can help the person they are mentoring set goals for tomorrow and develop her or his gifts today. If both parent and child are diligent about honing these gifts, God will be able to use them to serve Him and others more fully in the future.

It should be noted that Jesus did not nag Peter to grow up, even after He called him a rock. Ephesians 6:4 offers advice to fathers—both natural and spiritual—to guide their children (which includes seeing their potential) without unduly criticizing them: "And you, fathers, do not provoke your children to wrath, but bring them up in the training and admonition of the Lord" (*NKJV*). Children will not reach their potential if parents demoralize them with unrealistic expectations or constant criticisms. A spiritual father should not be too quick to correct his son's mistakes or expect too much too soon (this obviously applies to a spiritual mother as well). Although honesty is important and spiritual parents should not overlook a fault if it hinders their spiritual children's walk with the Lord, spiritual parents should be slow to barge in and correct. Sometimes a spiritual parent may see a weakness and realize that the best way for the son or daughter to overcome it is to discover it him- or herself. In that case, the spiritual parent simply ensures that he or she is available to help process and deal with the weakness when it surfaces to the son's or daughter's attention. Instead of pointing out the fault too quickly, the spiritual parent prays for and builds up the spiritual child with encouraging words, refusing to dishearten the growing spiritual son or daughter with nagging and criticism.

Nurture Trust

Trust is the cornerstone of a successful spiritual parenting relationship, which grows in small increments and accumulates over time. Trust begins when the spiritual daughter or son is assured of the spiritual parent's love. I heard someone once say that God calls us to a higher love than the world demands, a love that does not wait for people to change. Spiritual mothers and fathers accept their spiritual children as they are, even as they gently encourage them to grow. An environment that allows the person who is being mentored to be him- or herself without fear of judgment or impatience on the spiritual parent's part must be provided. A commitment to the confidentiality of discussions is also a necessity. Only then can trust blossom.

In His day-to-day life, Jesus modeled the character traits for His followers that we should seek to emulate: compassion, wisdom, honesty and purity, among others. He knew that spontaneous interaction is important when nurturing trust. Because growth and maturity are more caught than taught, informal conversation and time together model the kingdom of God by showing how Christianity works in real life. A spiritual mother should allow her spiritual daughter to observe her in real-life family relationships—how she handles crisis situations, such as when her teenager comes in past curfew or when her husband is working late *again*. A spiritual son should witness how his spiritual father functions in his everyday world and witness first-hand how he deals with life's quirky situations, such as how he deals with drivers on the roadway or the different personalities on the bowling team. Spiritual moms and dads can invite their spiritual children over for meals and make them feel a part of their natural family. They can hang out together, golf together, shop together, eat together, fish together, bake together, weed the garden together or attend a sporting event together. As time is spent rubbing shoulders with each other, trust slowly blooms and bears fruit.

Be Available

Jesus was completely approachable and fully accessible to His disciples for three years, and His disciples grew spiritually mature under His tutelage. When spiritual parents follow the model of Jesus, they make themselves accessible and available to their spiritual children.

Today's society, especially in the Western world, encourages us to be individualistic and selfish with our time. We fill our calendars to the maximum with work-related tasks and generous time slots for recreation and taking care of number one. A loving spiritual parent selflessly refuses to fall into this egocentric trap.

A spiritual parenting relationship is marked by its liberality, because spiritual fathers and mothers give of their time generously and sacrificially, just as Jesus did with His disciples. With open hearts and hands, they purposefully take their spiritual children under their wings. It is not always comfortable to make oneself available at 2 A.M. for a crisis phone call, but a spiritual parent graciously takes it in stride because he or she loves the spiritual child.

According to family counselor John M. Drescher, our children need our time. He tells the story of a son who was watching his father polish the car. After observing the time and careful attention lavished on the automobile, the boy asked:

"Dad, your car's worth a lot, isn't it?"

"Yes," his dad replied, "it cost a lot. It pays to take care of it. When I trade the car in, it will be worth more if I take care of it."

After some silence the son said, "I guess I'm not worth very much, am I?"[2]

The son's sad comment reveals that actions speak louder than words. Likewise, a spiritual mother knows that when she invests her life in nurturing her spiritual daughter, the daughter will grow up to be spiritually productive. And when a spiritual father spends time with his son, the son knows that he is worth a great deal.

On the flipside, red flags should go up if a spiritual daughter or son expects too much time and energy from her or his spiritual parent. Expecting a spiritual parent to be available whenever and wherever the spiritual child has a need is unrealistic. The amount of time spent together in a spiritual parenting relationship should be more or less determined in advance.

A husband complaining that his wife's spiritual daughter gets more attention than he does, or a spiritual parent's natural child saying something like, "Dad, why is Ryan here all the time?" is a warning sign that the person being mentored is expecting too much of the spiritual parent's time. Spiritual fathers and mothers cannot be at the beck and call of their spiritual child's whims to the detriment of his or her own family. Spiritual mentoring *is* a commitment of time and energy, but options should be explored to make *efficient* and *effective* use of time. The quality of time spent together is more important than the quantity.

Impart What You Have to Give

When Jesus shared with His disciples what He considered most important in preparation for His death, He spoke these words:

> As the Father has loved me, so have I loved you. Now re-
> main in my love. If you obey my commands, you will
> remain in my love, just as I have obeyed my Father's com-
> mands and remain in his love. I have told you this so that
> my joy may be in you and that your joy may be complete.
> My command is this: Love each other as I have loved you.
> Greater love has no one than this, that he lay down his
> life for his friends. You are my friends if you do what I
> command. I no longer call you servants, because a ser-
> vant does not know his master's business. Instead, I have
> called you friends, for everything that I learned from my
> Father I have made known to you (John 15:9-15).

Jesus had passed on to the disciples assembled in the Upper Room everything the Father had given Him. It was His joy to impart to His friends everything He had to give.

Spiritual parents will experience the true joy of mentoring when they take what they have and impart it to their spiritual children. "Impart" means to give another what one is or has. Through the spiritual parents' teaching and influence, an impartation of everything the spiritual parents are willing to give is conferred on those that they mentor.

Natural parents want to see their children grow into maturity. They teach them by example, because they know that if they do a good job, their lineage will be prosperous and healthy. The parenting process has at its core the intention of raising healthy children who can produce more productive and healthy children.

The heart's cry of spiritual fathers and mothers is similar. Their goal is for their children to reach their full potential as men and women of God. In spiritual mentoring relationships, all this takes place in an atmosphere of patient love and acceptance, without judgment or fear of rejection. It happens naturally and easily by example and modeled behavior as spiritual parents initiate, build and release their family of spiritual children, imparting everything they have to give.

This is true spiritual parenting as modeled for us by Jesus.

Key Questions for Practical Application

1. In what specific ways does the Jesus model apply to your life?
2. How does a spectator mentality cause stagnant and limited growth in the Church?
3. What can you do to provide an environment that enables spiritual children to mature without fearing your judgment or impatience with them?

Developing as a Spiritual Parent

Key: You need to develop the kind of spiritual parenting relationship your spiritual son or daughter needs.

Les is on the pastoral team of one of our DOVE International churches in Pennsylvania. He says he is indebted to a man who encouraged him when he encountered Christ as a young adult:

My life was dramatically changed when I came to Christ. I started attending a church, but a few months later, after attending every church meeting and activity I could find, I still felt disconnected and insecure in my faith. Everyone else seemed to have it all together. Sure, I was learning a lot and had made many friends, but initially I had no one I really trusted to ask those soul-searching questions that nagged and threatened to destroy my newly found faith. I really was at a loss to know how to apply the truth of God's Word to my life.

If it had not been for a 77-year-old spiritual father from my church who took a special interest in me, I would have probably thrown in the towel. But this elderly man patiently answered my searching questions and sacrificially devoted hours explaining the Scriptures to me. In addition, he spent time just being my friend. Through the mentoring of my first spiritual dad, I was firmly planted in God's Word and grew spiritually strong.

I am convinced that this man and the subsequent spiritual fathers the Lord brought into my life were key factors in my maturing process in Christ. I clearly remember the night one of my spiritual fathers called me on the phone and asked me to go with him to pray for a sick man from our church. I had never done this before. As we walked into the man's home, my spiritual father handed me a bottle of oil, so we could pray for him, anointing him according to James chapter 5. I opened the bottle and dumped the whole bottle of oil on him. The poor guy had oil running down over his face onto his shoulders. I almost drowned him!

On the way home that evening, my spiritual father gently advised me, "Lester, next time, go a bit light on the oil!" He treated me like a son and loved me unconditionally, even when I made mistakes. I learned by practical demonstration the importance of training others by example.

These caring father-son relationships carried me through my first years as a Christian. My spiritual fathers passed the baton to me, depositing in me a desire to be a father to others. I am so grateful.[1]

Les determined he would take the biblical challenge to give his life to others, following his spiritual fathers' examples. Today, Les is a pastor who challenges all believers to demonstrate the love of God in action by developing vital relationships with younger Christians, and in doing so, he perpetuates a legacy of spiritual parenting.

Different Kinds of Spiritual Parenting

Les's first spiritual father focused on grounding him in the Word and answering his questions about what living a Christian life truly encompasses. One of his later spiritual fathers helped Les develop his gifts and spread his ministry wings. Like Les's different spiritual fathers, spiritual parents may be involved in different types of spiritual parenting relationships—as disciplers, coaches, teachers, counselors, and so on—with their spiritual daughters and sons.

Discipler

If spiritual children are new to the faith, spiritual fathers or mothers will want to disciple these young Christians. That means spending time studying the Bible together, answering questions about Scripture and praying together. The role of spiritual parents in this relationship is to ground the new spiritual children in the basics of the Christian faith, laying the foundation for fruitful lives following Jesus.

The first few years after our cell-based church started, we discovered the pressing need for a basic biblical foundation course to help spiritual mothers and fathers disciple new believers. To meet that need, I wrote 12 books that presented basic Christian foundations that could be taught systematically from the Scriptures.[2] The books are geared especially for spiritual parenting relationships, especially relationships with younger Christians, and are complete with teaching outlines and questions broken down into increments of time. The response we got from users of these Christian doctrine books was amazing. Within a few short years, over 250,000 of the books were distributed throughout the Body of Christ. God's people are hungry for practical discipling tools to use in spiritual parenting relationships.

New believers need to become grounded in the Word of God. Discipler-parents are those who relationally reach out to those they mentor to teach them biblical truths. They take responsibility for maintaining accountability with their spiritual children until they grow to maturity and become disciples themselves who then go on to disciple others.

Coach

Coaching is often described as helping people clarify their goals and develop strategies for achieving those goals. As coaches, spiritual mothers and fathers share their skills, knowledge and expertise to help their spiritual children grow in a particular direction, guiding those they are mentoring through the process of setting and reaching goals. Coaching is goal-oriented and may focus on almost any area of life—business, career, family, health, personal growth, spirituality, financial responsibility, and so on. Wise parents will also help their children to develop and sharpen their ministry skills and become more effective in ministry to those they will parent spiritually. Coach-parents help individuals gain the results they want in the way they want, and they build on their strengths and resources.

Teacher

Spiritual children may need instruction in areas as diverse as leadership development, cross-cultural evangelism or conflict resolution. Spiritual fathers and mothers who are teacher-parents are those who can organize information and present it so that their sons and daughters learn it rapidly. This information can be imparted in a training course, a small group or person to person. Regardless of the setting, teacher-parents challenge their children to use the information and make it relevant to their lives.

Counselor

The central focus of spiritual mother's and father's function as counselor-parents is timely counsel and perspective for the lives of their spiritual daughters and sons. These wise parents act as sounding boards for those they mentor to process new ideas or difficult situations, and they impart hope when their children's world seems overwhelming. Counselor-parents listen carefully and help their children avoid making serious misjudgments as they work through issues in their past or present. They give specific advice for specific situations.

Group

Some spiritual parents maintain a one-on-one relationship with their spiritual children and also mentor them in a small-group setting, where they gather together with other people to pray and study the Bible. It can be beneficial for spiritual children to have healthy interaction in a group setting while spiritual parents observe and train them. A group, however, cannot take the place of a person-to-person relationship that occurs when a parent sits down with the one they are mentoring face-to-face and intentionally takes the time to listen and really sense what the child is feeling.

Please note that small groups are especially effective when the time comes to release your spiritual children. In groups, everyone has an opportunity to be a spiritual father and mother and train the next generation.

Reverse Mentoring

A reverse-mentoring relationship is a twist on a traditional spiritual parent relationship, because in this case, it is the spiritual child who teaches the spiritual parent something new or valuable, rather than the other way around. The relationship involves both giving and getting feedback, but this time it is the parent who is the one tapping into the wisdom of the spiritual child.

The concept of reverse mentoring, or reverse parenting, first gained widespread attention in the late 1990s when a former chairman of GE instructed several hundred of his top managers to work with younger employees to learn about the Internet.[3] He realized that the younger generation was light years ahead of the older generation in their knowledge of technology. The outgrowth these kinds of relationships forged was quite productive, and the sharing of knowledge seemed to work both ways.

In his book *Off-Road Disciplines*, Earl Creps encourages the older generation to go "off road" and work to develop reverse-mentoring relationships. He says a reverse-mentoring relationship is "a very specific form of friendship in which the junior instructs the senior, not as a replacement for other forms of mentoring but as an essential complement to them."[4] Creps goes on to say:

> Reverse mentoring opens up the possibility of a relationship in which both participants simultaneously teach

and learn, each making the other an adopted peer. "As iron sharpens iron, so one man sharpens another" [(Prov. 27:17)]. Strictly one-way mentoring (upward or downward) resembles iron sharpening wood: all the power is on the side of the person whittling the other. . . . But with iron on both sides, each can be sharpened or conformed into the image of Christ through the work of the Spirit in the relationship.

A reciprocal relationship between young and old holds the potential for a . . . partnership . . . in a way that no other method can produce.[5]

For example, young people have a lot to teach the older generation about computers, iPods, text messaging and social media, because the younger generation grew up with these technologies and are much more proficient in using them. Right now my tech-savvy son-in-law is reverse parenting me as I learn computer skills. Whenever I want my computer to perform a task I don't know how to make it perform, he comes to the rescue.

Some of Paul's instructions to Timothy seem to have reverse parenting in view, such as, "Do not rebuke an older man harshly, but exhort him as if he were your father. Treat younger men as brothers, older women as mothers, and younger women as sisters" (1 Tim. 5:1-2). Paul knew that when generations work together, they realize how much they need each other. Their different perspectives allow a sharing of knowledge that would never happen otherwise.

Combination Roles

Of course, the role of the spiritual parent can have all these characteristics rolled up into one. I have had spiritual parenting relationships in which I helped cultivate a new believer's faith in Christ, coached him in family and career development, trained him in leadership development and imparted advice. I was a discipler, coach, teacher and counselor at different points in the relationship, according to what my spiritual son needed.

The Fundamentals of Spiritual Parenting

Whatever shape the spiritual parenting relationship takes, there are a few basics that are nonnegotiables.

Praying

Prayer must be woven into the very fabric of the spiritual parenting relationship. Praying for our spiritual children will wrap them in the Lord's protection and increase our sensitivity to their spiritual growth. Spiritual parenting cannot be just another item on our to-do list. Christians have enough meetings to attend and things to do already! Developing a spiritual parenting relationship must be something the Lord imparts to each of us personally, and it must be birthed in prayer. We need to pray initially that the Lord will lead us to the right relationship, and then we need to pray diligently every day for our spiritual daughters and sons. Remember that "the effective, fervent prayer of a righteous man [or woman] avails much" (Jas. 5:16, *NKJV*).

Paul wrote in Galatians 4:19 that he labored "in the pains of childbirth" for the Galatian church for Christ to be formed in them. Much of his "labor" was in prayer for those believers. He invested a lot of time in those Christians, whom he affectionately called his "children," and he expected that each one would grow up spiritually strong.

Job was another praying man. He rose early every morning and offered a sacrifice for each of his children (see Job 1:5). Jesus was the ultimate spiritual parent, and He prayed for His spiritual children so that they would not fail. In the Gospel of Luke we read that He prayed for Simon Peter out of His special concern for his spirit. Jesus knew that Peter was about to deny Him: "Simon, Simon, Satan has asked to sift you as wheat. But I have prayed for you, Simon, that your faith may not fail" (Luke 22:31-32). Jesus is at the right hand of the Father interceding, not only for the world in general, but also for us individually (see Rom. 8:34).

Ibrahim Omondi from Kenya, who oversees DOVE International churches in East Africa and serves as a spiritual father to church leaders in various nations, describes how prayer with a spiritual father brought him spiritual maturity:

Those who had discipled me as a young Christian had long moved out of my life. I was left on my own until at a Bible school, I met an elderly professor who asked if I could pray with him regularly. Our weekly prayer meetings soon took on the form of a father-son relationship. I loved it. I recognized what I had missed throughout my Christian walk. I was able to open up in prayer. The deepest secrets of my life found no hiding place. I felt a new sense of security, love and deep humility.

We must pray specific prayers for our spiritual children. We must pray that they will run to God and hunger for God's Word. And we must pray that they will learn to resist temptation and flee from it.

Hearing from God

Not only should spiritual parents diligently pray for their spiritual children, but they should also teach them to hear from God for themselves. Spiritual sons and daughters will grow to maturity as they learn to hear and discern God's voice.

Jesus told His disciples one day that sheep follow the shepherd "because they know his voice" (John 10:4). How do they know his voice? Because they spend time with him, know him and have learned from experience that he can be trusted. In the same way, to hear God's voice clearly, we must have a growing love relationship with God and trust Him. It's that simple. The better we get to know God, the better we will recognize His voice. Your spiritual children need to learn to hear the voice of God, and you, as a spiritual mother or father, can help them learn to hear Him speak by sharing your own personal life experiences.

The Bible is filled with examples of common and ordinary people who heard the voice of our mighty God. Adam and Eve walked and talked with God in the Garden of Eden. The Lord startled Moses from within a flaming bush in the desert when He called him to deliver the Israelites out of the bondage in Egypt. God advised Joshua to be strong and courageous, and gave David fresh strategies for each battle against his enemies. Through the angel Gabriel, the Lord told Mary she would be the mother of Jesus. By His voice speaking from heaven, God affirmed Jesus at His baptism, and Paul was totally transformed by the Lord's voice on the Damascus road. When God's people hear His voice, lives are changed.

God delights in revealing Himself to us. He promises to answer if we call on Him: "Call to me and I will answer you and tell you great and unsearchable things you do not know" (Jer. 33:3). When we pray, we engage ourselves in conversation with God and God responds.

At the same time that we teach our spiritual children to listen for God's voice, we also need to share with our spiritual daughters and sons that everyone at one time or another struggles to hear God's voice. We want to do what the Lord wants us to do, and we know we serve a living God who speaks to us, yet we all struggle when we do not hear God as clearly as we would like. It may seem as if we are trying to tune in to a weak radio signal with a lot of static. Despite our troubles hearing, God wants to speak to us, even more than we desire to hear from Him.

Another point to remind spiritual children of is the times when we think we have heard the Lord's voice and we respond to it only to find that we were wrong. Instead of pressing in to find out how and why we "missed it," we may hesitate to step out in faith the next time. Though we may wish God would send a 10-foot-tall angel dressed in white so that we would have no doubt that it is God's voice we are hearing, I believe He often teaches us by allowing us to stumble through a series of trials and errors.

Even Jesus' disciples did not always recognize God's voice. When Jesus joined two of His disciples on the road to Emmaus and began to talk to them, they didn't recognize Him, even though they had walked with Him, talked with Him and eaten meals with Him for the past three years (see Luke 24:13-32). Perhaps they were so immersed in the details of the dark events of the past few days that they couldn't hear clearly. I think there is a good chance, however, that they did not see Jesus because they simply did not expect to see Him. He appeared to them in an unfamiliar form at an unexpected time, and their ears remained closed.

Before we criticize these disciples, we each must ask ourselves, *How often do I experience the same loss of hearing today?* Could it be that the Lord sometimes speaks to us in ways that are unfamiliar to us, and we don't recognize His voice? We lament that we can't hear Him speak, but in reality He may have been speaking all along. Could it be that our understanding of hearing His voice is limited? Maybe we have preconceived ideas about how God will speak or not speak to us, and those ideas keep us from hearing God when He speaks.

The Bible gives us many examples of the enormous range of ways God can speak to us: the inner witness of the Holy Spirit, His Word, prayer, circumstances, other people, dreams or visions. The Lord may speak to us by using His audible voice; however, don't expect God's audible voice to be the common way He will speak! God's voice often blends into a melodic harmony to which we have to tune in.[6]

I'm convinced that we should not get too selective about how we expect the Lord to speak to us. Instead, we should stay open for the Lord to speak to us in any way He desires. He may be speaking to us every day in ways we simply miss because of what *we* expect. We need to remember for ourselves and we need to teach our spiritual children that "God does speak—now one way, now another—though man may not perceive it" (Job 33:14).

Expecting Accountability

Christians find support through accountability, so this should be a given in every spiritual parenting relationship. Accountability is a way for us to check up on each other so that we stay on a safe path and remain responsible for our actions.

What exactly is accountability? Personal accountability is finding out from God what He wants us to do and then asking someone to hold us accountable to follow through on those behaviors. If a spiritual daughter wants to be held accountable to her spiritual mother for a certain area in her life that needs support, it doesn't mean the mother tells her what to do. The spiritual mother does not control the actions and decisions of her daughter. Instead, she forms a partnership with her spiritual daughter that results in good choices and personal growth. The daughter makes the final decision about what she will do in any given situation. Spiritual parents point others to Jesus; because in the end, each person is responsible for his or her own decisions.

The truth of Galatians 4:2, that children need "guardians and trustees," does not mean spiritual parents stand guard over their spiritual children. They don't peer over their children's shoulders, waiting for them to make wrong moves. Rather, the parents help those they mentor become self-disciplined and self-motivated so that they are not reliant on the pushing and prodding of their mentors. Spiritual parenting is not to be used to get the spiritual children to do what the parents want them to do or to serve the ambitions of their spiritual parents. Instead, parents must help those they mentor to discern God's will for their lives while holding them accountable to carry out His will.

Normally a spiritual parenting relationship is characterized by deep friendship and trust, so if spiritual children seem to be making unwise decisions or are participating in destructive behaviors, the parents who express concerns will be heard. Spiritual parents should not condemn but instead confront their children with love and respect. In this way, they will be more likely to be teachable and open to input.

Good spiritual parents are excellent listeners and are willing to give advice and provide guidance. On the other hand, they are also willing to sometimes stand back and let the children proceed on their own, if the spiritual parents discern that this approach will be better in the long run. One spiritual daughter says this about her spiritual mother: "My spiritual mom has a way of knowing when to push and challenge, when to allow me the time to savor my accomplishments or mourn my disappointments. She knows when to let me make my own decisions and when to guide me step by step through certain circumstances."

Spurring Achievement
Closely tied to expecting accountability is spurring spiritual children on to achieving their goals. Spiritual parents need to ask

their spiritual sons or daughters questions to encourage them to reach new spiritual heights:

- "How is your relationship with Jesus?"
- "How has God been speaking to you through His Word?"
- "What are some areas in your life that God is pressing His finger on?"
- "What are some areas of concern the Father has placed in you to be praying about?"
- "Has your thought life been pure?"
- "What sin has tempted you this week?"
- "What struggles are you having in your life?"
- "In what ways have you stepped out in faith lately?"
- "Have you shared your faith this week?"
- "Are you serving others in love?"
- "What was your greatest joy this week?"
- "What was your biggest disappointment this week?"
- "What do you see yourself doing five or ten years in the future?"
- "What gifts do you possess that you feel you are not using right now?"
- "What is your most passionate pursuit?"
- "What is your most intense longing?"
- "How can I help you fulfill what the Lord has called you to do?"

For spiritual children who are married, these questions may be added:

- "How is your relationship with your spouse?"
- "Have you been on a date night lately?"
- "Do you take the necessary time to communicate?"

Spiritual sons and daughters can also be asked about their relationships with their natural children or with their natural parents or with their church. Questions similar to these will motivate them to be thoughtful about their daily interactions and help them to be more like Christ. Of course, we should not bombard our spiritual sons or daughters with all these questions at one time! And it is never wise to preach at our spiritual children by using these types of questions as leverage. Those that we mentor do not need us to lecture them. Many of these personal issues will come up naturally in our conversations as the friendships develop.

Being a Servant

Servanthood must be the crux of spiritual parenting relationships. Leading through service releases spiritual children to be all they can be, empowering them to grow. I like the way Tom Marshall says it in *Understanding Leadership*: "The servant leader is willing to share power with others so that they are empowered. That is, they become freer, more autonomous, more capable, and therefore more powerful."[7] A servant leader knows that the more authority there is to spread around, the more people there are who have authority. When the parenting relationship centers on servanthood, people in the relationship are empowered to use their own gifts and abilities. As I have emphasized several times, good spiritual parents release their spiritual children to go and do it themselves! I can't stress this enough. Approaching every parenting relationship with the attitude of a servant will enable us to hand the ministry over to the children being trained.

The Levites were instructed to serve in the tent of meeting from age 25 until they were age 50, when they were required to retire and assist the next generation of priests (see Num. 8:23-26). They were called to pass on the ministry to those they had been fathering. In this same way, be a Levite. Allow your spiritual daughters and sons to try new things for the first time and succeed. This is how "the equipping of the saints for the work of ministry" is supposed to work (Eph. 4:12). This kind of apprenticeship-modeling-discipleship-rolled-up-in-one is how new generations of spiritual parents are trained! As spiritual parents, we empower our spiritual daughters and sons to become spiritual parents themselves.

Showing Vulnerability

At the Last Supper, Jesus took off His outer garment and knelt down to wash the disciples' feet, saying, "I have set you an example that you should do as I have done for you" (John 13:15). Before an individual can serve others, she or he must take off her or his "outer garment." Although an outer garment is usually cast off when serious work is about to begin, the outer garment can also be regarded as a metaphor for the "Sunday-best behavior" that must be cast off in order to enter into a real family relationship. Sometimes an outer garment is a cover-up to hide vulnerabilities. We don't want others to see our weaknesses, so we keep our outer garments pulled around us, intact and stiff, getting in the way of real relationships.

Opening up our lives to others is a complex and risky proposition. But honesty is humbling and liberating. A performance mentality will go out the door when we share our real, uncloaked lives with others. Uncloaked, we will serve, not because we think it is required of us, but because we love as God loved us.

Effective spiritual parenting involves a commitment to vulnerability—a willingness to open our lives to one another and an acceptance of other people without reservation. Spiritual parents are not afraid to take the risk of sharing their lives openly with other people. Transparency leads to intimacy. If parents are free to reveal their true feelings, their children learn to open up, too. Spiritual mentors do not hesitate to talk about their failures as well as their successes. Other people identify with such open spiritual parents when they see the parents' weaknesses, because everyone has them! Spiritual mothers and fathers are each willing to say, "Follow me as I, a sinful human being, follow Christ."

Early in our marriage, LaVerne and I went to see a marriage counselor because we recognized that our marriage relationship was empty on the inside. We were no longer connecting emotionally, and we both wondered if we had married the wrong person. Being open about this time in our lives has encouraged many married couples to get the help they need when facing a crisis in their marriage.

Spiritual sons or daughters will not think less of their spiritual parents when they know their struggles—they will just be relieved that they, the children, are normal! If they know their spiritual parents are human, they won't be tempted to put their spiritual parents up on pedestals. And neither will those that they mentor feel alone in their own struggles.

For example, Jane, one of the spiritual daughters I know, described the relief she felt when "the giant of a spiritual woman" she looked to as a spiritual parent revealed that even her 30-year marriage experienced bumps in the road—times when she and her husband did not see eye to eye. "Just hearing her admit to her unspiritual thoughts helped me to see that she was learning to live in the grace of God in her marriage too, and I was not alone in my problems," said Jane. The younger woman was relieved and encouraged because her spiritual mother dared to say, "I am committed to Jesus Christ, and I'm going to be honest with you about how I struggle sometimes to live my Christian life."

If we want our spiritual daughters and sons to be open with us, we need to be open with them. My friend Carl was leading a small group of believers in his home, and he asked if anyone had any needs the group could pray about. The room was silent. So Carl opened up his heart and began to share some personal struggles and asked the group members to pray for him. He told me that what happened next was amazing: Within a few minutes, everybody in the room spoke up about a problem and asked for prayer. Carl opened the door to genuine sharing by modeling openness and vulnerability.

Timing is vital to keep in mind when it comes to fostering vulnerability and expecting people to open their lives to us. We earn the right to speak into people's lives, and earning takes time. As long as the earth remains, Genesis 8:22 tells us, there will be seasons. Life is filled with seasons of time. I would never think to swim in a lake during our cold Pennsylvanian wintertime; it is simply the wrong season to do it. Likewise, in the summertime, my snow shovel is put away; I don't need it until the winter piles heaps of snow on my driveway.

God's timing is paramount. His timetable, or schedule, is much better than ours, and He is much more concerned about the process than the end result. God sees a beautiful diamond in each one of us, but it takes time for Him to cut out the impurities in our lives so that we can sparkle and reflect Jesus. Anything the Lord can find in our lives that does not look like Jesus must go.

As a part of this process, the Lord uses relationships with others. As we are transparent and open with the believers closest to us, including our spiritual children, we are refined. The more we are open with those we parent, the more they will be open with us. As we both share from our hearts and challenge one another to grow closer to Jesus, we shine and reflect His image more and more clearly.

If spiritual parents focus on these major points—praying, hearing from God, expecting accountability, spurring achievement, being a servant and showing vulnerability—a solid, stable foundation will be laid for growing, healthy relationships.

Key Questions for Practical Application

1. How does a spiritual child learn to apply God's Word to her or his life?
2. What benefits have you experienced from reverse parenting? If you haven't had a reverse-mentoring relationship, what do you imagine you could learn from a younger person?
3. What are a few specific ways you can use to teach your spiritual daughter or son to hear God's voice?

Making Decisions as a Spiritual Parent

Key: You should help your spiritual daughter or son make wise decisions.

No matter what kind of spiritual parent you are—discipler, coach, teacher, counselor, group or reverse—it is inevitable that you will be called on to guide your spiritual children in making decisions. This means, obviously, that you as a spiritual parent need to be wise in making your own decisions before you can pass on wise counsel to your daughter or son. How can you make wise decisions according to a biblical pattern and pass on this pattern to the next generation?

A look at the first-century Church in Acts 15 will reveal what they did when they faced a crisis and needed to make a decision; and from their example, we can learn how spiritual mothers and fathers can make decisions that honor the Lord and value each member of their family.

The Early Church Model for Making Decisions

In Acts 15, we are given a model for healthy decision making. This chapter of Acts describes a particular crisis that arose when a group of Jewish believers from the Jerusalem church came to visit the church in Antioch because they objected to Gentiles coming into the Church without submitting to the Jewish rite of circumcision. Subsequently, Paul and Barnabas were sent from Antioch along with the other apostles and elders to serve on a council in Jerusalem because of the heated debate that ensued:

> So, being sent on their way by the church, [Paul and Barnabas] passed through Phoenicia and Samaria, describing the conversion of the Gentiles; and they caused great joy to all the brethren. And when they had come to Jerusalem, they were received by the church and the apostles and the elders; and they reported all things that God had done with them. But some of the sect of the Pharisees who believed rose up, saying, "It is necessary to circumcise them, and to command them to keep the law of Moses" (Acts 15:3-5, NKJV).

When Paul and Barnabas met with the leaders and then the apostles and elders in Jerusalem, they shared what they had experienced with the Gentiles who had received Christ. Then, because some believers felt that the new converts should be circumcised, there was quite a bit of wrangling and argument from those on both sides of the question. Finally, Peter rose up and said to them:

> Men and brethren, you know that a good while ago God chose among us, that by my mouth the Gentiles should hear the word of the gospel and believe. So God, who knows the heart, acknowledged them by giving them the Holy Spirit, just as He did to us, and made no distinction between us and them, purifying their hearts by faith (Acts 15:7-9, NKJV).

Peter reminded these Jewish believers that they had been saved by faith and faith alone, just as the Gentile believers had been saved. When he was finished speaking, "the multitude kept silent and listened to Barnabas and Paul declaring how many miracles and wonders God had worked through them among the Gentiles" (Acts 15:12). After Peter, Paul and Barnabas had their say, James, the head elder and apostolic leader of the Jerusalem church, spoke up (the Early Church leaders trusted James because they were in his field of authority and responsibility).

First, James reviewed what he had heard from various leaders throughout the meeting. Second, he quoted from the Scriptures. Finally, he spoke in favor of accepting the uncircumcised Gentiles: "Therefore I judge that we should not trouble those from among the Gentiles who are turning to God" (Acts 15:19, *NKJV*). The apostles, elders and the whole congregation agreed with James's wise words and decided to send delegates to Antioch and throughout the other city-churches to report the decision with an "acceptance letter" (see Acts 15:23-29). A church doctrinal issue was resolved!

Principles for Making Decisions

I believe this Early Church issue was resolved because God's leaders followed three biblical decision-making principles:

1. God speaks through a leader.
2. God speaks through the team.
3. God speaks through His people.

Looking at the Acts 15 story carefully, we see the combined strengths of these three godly decision-making principles at work, and I believe that these three principles can help us make wise decisions at any level of leadership. Trouble often comes when one of these principles is given greater precedence than the others. Practicing only one of these principles is like driving a car in a rut on the side of the road rather than utilizing the entire road; the result is lopsided. Similarly, a spiritual parent who leads by giving precedence to only one of these principles leads in a lopsided manner, often making poor decisions. These three principles are meant to complement each other and work in relationship with one another.

To better understand the dynamics between all three principles, think for a minute about the options a natural family has if they utilize one or more of these principles while planning a vacation. Let's say the Mancini family wants to make a decision about where to spend their summer vacation. Who should make the decision? Should Dad make a decision to go on a fishing vacation without taking the rest of his family into consideration? Should Mom and Dad discuss the issue thoroughly and then give up the idea entirely when they cannot agree? Should the children have a say and then have all family members vote to decide by democratic majority where to go? Or is there a better way?

1. God Speaks Through a Leader

God always calls and anoints someone to lead the way. Although God may speak His vision and direction through many people, one person is always appointed by the Lord to be the primary spokesperson for the vision. That one person has a greater responsibility than the others on the team to see the vision fulfilled. James was the head elder and apostle at Jerusalem who held this role. You could say that James was the father, or primary vision carrier, for the group. He was the one who heard what the Lord was saying through the entire team and declared what He believed the Lord was saying to the Church.

Both the Old and New Testaments give numerous examples of a "leader who leads the way" principle: Adam, Noah, Abraham, Joseph, Deborah, Gideon, David, Jesus, Peter, James, Paul—the list goes on and on. Moses asked the Lord to appoint a man who would succeed him as leader over the Israelites (see Num. 27:16). According to Acts 13:1-4, Barnabas and Saul were sent out with a team to evangelize and plant new churches. But by verse 13 of that chapter, the Bible says that "Paul and his party" went to the next city. In other words, Paul had clearly become the primary leader of the team.

In the corporate world, the leader of a business is often known as the Chief Executive Officer (CEO). A CEO is responsible for the vision and general oversight of the company: what goes on within its doors, how it will grow and what will be its overall image. The CEO has authority to make decisions that affect the future of the company, and the position of CEO is usually equated with power and prestige.

A spiritual leader, on the other hand, leads in a totally different manner. Though the spiritual leader is also in a position of authority and is responsible for the people the Lord has placed within his or her care, the leader does not lead as a domineering CEO. A spiritual leader leads as a parent who supports his or her spiritual children in order to see the *children* fulfill *their* dreams and visions. The parent encourages his or her children to hear from God and make their own decisions rather than always handing down decisions made at the top.

A misguided CEO often *uses* people, but a spiritual father or mothers *serves* people. A true Christian leader's rights decrease as he or she takes up his or her position of authority and as responsibilities increase. The spiritual leader's rights decrease, because Christian leadership involves not power or prestige but servanthood, which is the mark of a leader deeply committed to the development of others. Servant leadership takes its example from Christ, the master leader, when He demonstrated that He "did not come to be served, but to serve" (Mark 10:45).

In a family, fathers should be willing to serve by making final decisions: "The husband is the head of the wife as Christ is the head of the church, his body, of which he is the Savior" (Eph. 5:23). In every team, there is always someone the Lord places as the leader of that team. In the case of the husband and wife, the Bible says the husband is the head of the wife. He's the one who is called to love his wife the same way Jesus Christ loves His Church and gave His life for it. The husband is also the one who is responsible to lead the process of decision making in the home. If a final decision must be made, he is responsible to make the decision in harmony with his family and in such a way that values them.

A few years ago, LaVerne and I came to a decision-making impasse regarding whether or not one of our children should be enrolled in a public school or a Christian school. We prayed and waited before the Lord for an answer, but we could not clearly hear the voice of the Lord. Finally LaVerne told me, "Honey, you are the head of our home, and I believe you will hear what the Lord is saying in this situation. I will honor your decision." In the end, the decision I felt God was leading me to make was the right one.

A godly father never throws his weight around as a leader. The apostle Paul, a respected leader in the Early Church, set an example for leaders: "We were not looking for praise from men, not from you or anyone else. As apostles of Christ we could have been a burden to you, but we were gentle among you, like a mother caring for her little children" (1 Thess. 2:6-7). Paul's letters were written from a loving spiritual parent's perspective, and he modeled the life of a servant to those he spiritually fathered.

Having said all this, there is a danger for those who lead solely through this principle of decision making: They become autocratic. Abuses of this kind of leadership breed Jim Jones-type cult leaders, husbands who abuse their wives, and spiritual parents who believe they have a right to tell their spiritual children what to do in a way that violates their personal authority and responsibility before the Lord. That's why the biblical process—the three principles of decision making—is so important. When used in tandem, the three principles bring harmony and peace to the entire family.

The Mancini family I mentioned earlier wants harmony and peace on their family vacation. They seek to honor each other in planning a vacation. If truth be told, Dad really, really wants to go on a fishing trip; and he knows that he can convince the rest of the family to go to the mountains, where he envisions lazy days spent by a cool stream with no distractions or work to do. But Dad also knows that going into a secluded spot in the mountains appeals only to him. It would yield grumpy and whiny children who would be bored and a wife who wouldn't get enough of his attention when he went off to the stream.

So as the leader of his family, Dad decides to give up his rights to make the decision by himself and instead decides to serve his family by first asking his wife and then his children for their suggestions for an enjoyable family vacation. Dad knows that his first priority is to talk to his wife. They are a team, and he wants to honor her and her wishes for the vacation.

2. God Speaks Through the Team

Although it is clear from Acts 15 that James was the primary leader in the Jerusalem church, it is important to see that James did not make decisions alone. The other apostles and elders met with him, and they worked together as a team to make a decision. James listened to what the Lord was saying through the entire team. The other apostles and elders were honored, because they were involved in the process and their input was valued. In this way, they were all able to confirm James's final decision.

In families, the Lord has called husbands and wives to submit to each other. God wants husbands and wives to be in unity and work as a team: "Submit to one another out of reverence for Christ" (Eph. 5:21).

We see this team leadership modeled many times in both the Old and New Testaments. Some leaders worked alone, but most often they served with a team of leaders who worked with them. Moses, Aaron and Miriam worked together as a team to lead the children of Israel from captivity in Egypt, as we read in Exodus. Acts 16:4 records that "apostles and elders" reached decisions, and in 1 Peter 5:1, the plural "elders" is used again. In Titus 1:5, Paul exhorts Titus to "appoint elders in every town," and we read that Paul and Barnabas "appointed elders for [the disciples] in each church" (Acts 14:23) to work as an eldership team.

Why is it so important to work together as a team? A primary leader has only so many gifts to lead God's people. According to the Bible, no matter how spiritual we think we are, "we know in part and we prophesy in part" (1 Cor. 13:9). The primary leader has only a portion of the Lord's wisdom. A team of leaders fills in the gaps for the primary leader's limitations and the limitations of other members of the team. A leader and his team listen to what the Lord says through each person on the team, and then the primary leader receives the grace to discern what the Lord is saying.

When a plane is in flight, the pilot, copilot and flight attendants all work together as a team to ensure that the passengers reach their destination safely and comfortably. But during take-off, landing and times of turbulence or a crisis, the other members of the team step back while the pilot takes clear leadership—and everyone on the plane is glad that the pilot does!

In 2001, (a few months before 9/11), I was on a flight that had just left the airport when a man seated in the rear of the plane caused a problem. He was visibly drunk and was pushing flight attendants, pulling the phone off the wall and cursing everyone in sight. Passengers seated in the rear of the plane moved out of their seats in fear for their safety.

One of the pilots came to the back of the plane to find out what was happening, and I met him in the aisle. "Could we help you, sir?" I asked.

"Yes, you can," the pilot said. "I need some strong men to help me handcuff that man before he hurts someone." I asked a few of my friends on board to help. We grabbed the man and held his hands behind his back as he was handcuffed, and then we pushed him back into his seat and secured him with his seatbelt. He struggled furiously to get out of his seat, so we held him down with rolled up blankets for the next few hours, making sure he did not rip the seat off the floor and hurt someone. Once the man was secure, the pilot went back to the cockpit. It was not your average flight! We were a team—the pilot, the flight attendants and me and my friends.

After a few hours, the pilot decided to make an emergency landing in Anchorage, Alaska, where the FBI escorted the troubled man off the plane. As the plane came to a stop at the airport, the captain came to the back of the plane. We had spent the past few hours working as a team, but we had been under his direction. When he showed up, we deferred to him. He was the primary leader, and we trusted him to make the right decisions for our safety.

After the plane was again in the air, the purser and flight attendants came and thanked us for helping. "Is there anything we can do for you?" they asked.

I told them with a smile, "I'd like upgrades for the rest of my life." They smiled and told me that was not possible, but they did give each of our team members an upgrade on our flight home (and we each received a free cup of coffee). We all felt like big shots. My daughter Katrina now tells my friends, "Dad will do anything for an upgrade!"

To get back to our imaginary family: Mr. Mancini knows that husbands and wives should submit to each other out of reverence for Christ. He knows that he cannot make a heavy-handed decision about their family vacation without discussing and planning it with his right-hand team member—his wife. His wife has valuable insights to bring to the table about what she and their children really would enjoy. She makes it known that she really would enjoy a vacation at the beach. Now they are looking at two very different landscapes—the mountains or the beach! How can they merge the two?

Dad and Mom take a few days to pray about the decision they must make. After praying, they both come to the conclusion that they could travel to a state park just on the edge of the state's coastline; there they could have the best of both worlds—a wooded campsite where Dad could fish in a freshwater stream and an ocean beach just a couple of miles drive away for Mom. They decide to present their combined vacation idea to their children to see what they have to say.

3. God Speaks Through His People

Wise parents listen to their children before making decisions that affect the family. Spiritual fathers take the time to hear the heart's cry of their spiritual children because they love them, believe the Lord speaks through them, and want to see them fulfill their destinies in God.

In Acts 6, we read about the choosing of leaders we sometimes call "deacons":

> The twelve gathered all the disciples together and said, "It would not be right for us to neglect the ministry of the word of God in order to wait on tables. Brothers, choose seven men from among you who are known to be full of the Spirit and of wisdom. We will turn this responsibility over to them and we will give our attention to prayer and the ministry of the word." This proposal pleased the whole group. They chose Stephen, a man full of faith and of the Holy Spirit; also Philip, Procorus, Nicanor, Timon, Parmenas, and Nicolas from Antioch, a convert to Judaism. They presented these men to the apostles, who prayed and laid their hands on them (Acts 6:2-6).

Who chose the deacons? Scripture says the brothers (in other words, the disciples) chose seven men, and the apostles appointed those seven.

During the council in Jerusalem regarding circumcision for the Gentile converts, James not only heard from his fellow apostles and elders, but he also heard many stories from Paul and Barnabas about the signs and wonders God had performed among the new Gentile believers. These stories were testimonies from God's people, and James took them into account when making his decision.

Wise leaders listen to what God says through His people. We spiritual parents are to receive input from those we serve before making a decision that affects them. In the church, wise leaders should publicly share the facts and receive godly input so as to leave no room for doubt and discontent among the congregation. In a natural or spiritual family, everyone's views and feelings should be taken into account. In this way, the members know that they are valued and cared for. Leaders must value the people they serve!

In regard to the Mancini family vacation, after the wife's opinion is discussed, the children are consulted. The children, who know just how much Dad loves to fish and how much Mom loves the ocean, listen to what Dad and Mom have to say about their upcoming vacation. They are reassured to know that Dad and Mom have come together in unity to try to make a decision that is best for the whole family. They also have their own opinions about what they would love to do on the vacation. An amusement park or water park somewhere near their vacation destination would be cool! They want more activity and action!

Dad and Mom listen to their kids. Together, they surf the Internet. *Voilà!* There is a water park and an amusement park within several miles of the campground they have thought to be their vacation destination. The decision is made. Dad has served his family by listening to them and their ideas. His family trusts him, because he did not try to make the decision on his own but instead wanted to see his family fulfill their dream vacation together.

Balancing the Principles of Decision Making

A leader must make the effort to focus on all three principles of decision-making in order to make balanced decisions. There are strengths in all three, and if a leader combines these strengths, he or she will experience tremendous unity in his or her sphere of influence.

Sometimes the analogy of *head*, *shoulders* and *body* is used to show the combined strength of all three principles. This body image helps to explain further how a spiritual leader works with others to hear what the Lord is saying, and if we look at Psalm 133, we'll see how and why.

Psalm 133 is a song about unity. At the point in biblical history when the psalm was written, Israel was united under one head: David. The blessing of this unity is imagined in the psalm as the fragrant, holy anointing oil poured upon the head of Aaron, the high priest. The oil was so plentiful that it ran down his face, onto his shoulders and over his garment: God pours out His wisdom on the head, which flows to the shoulders and onto the body.

Applying this analogy to balanced decision making, the head (primary leader) of every team must be properly attached to the shoulders (the others on the team) and the body (the people) through God-ordained relationships of trust and affirmation. If the head is appropriately attached to the shoulders by servanthood, prayer and proper communication, and if the shoulders properly support and affirm the head, there will be unity; and God will command a blessing as indicated in Psalm 133. God pours out His grace and anointing to the primary leader of the team so that the leader hears what God is saying through the entire team.

However, if the head is stretched too far from the shoulders—that is, the primary leader does not honor the team—and makes decisions in an autocratic style, the shoulders (the team) and the body (the people) experience a pain in the neck! By the same token, if the head is forced down through a lack of honor from the shoulders or the body, nobody will get very far. Unless there is trust established between team members and team leaders, decisions cannot be made effectively.

The head is committed to value the shoulders and the
body for good decision making. Wise leaders who are in roles
of authority will also pursue authentic accountability relationships with spiritual fathers or mothers who the Lord has
placed in their lives. This will help leaders avoid the absolute-
authority trap. (For a complete discussion of how these principles apply to church leadership, read *The Biblical Role of Elders
for Today's Church.*[1])

When God's people "live together in unity . . . the LORD be-
stows his blessing" (Ps. 133).

Passing on the Principles

Once wise spiritual parents have adopted the three biblical
principles into their decision making, the parents let their spiritual children see those principles being applied to their lives.
The principles need to be discussed with the children so that the
spiritual sons and daughters begin to identify how decisions that
affect the spiritual family are made.

When it comes time for our sons or daughters to make decisions, we need to help them apply the principles to their own
lives. They need to be encouraged to seek the input of everyone
impacted by the decision, to pray for the Lord's guidance and
direction, and then to move forward in confidence.

The key to all decision making is knowing that only the Lord
can give us wisdom for making decisions. We cannot lean on
our own understanding, as the writer of Proverbs admonishes
us: "Trust in the LORD with all your heart and lean not on your
own understanding; in all your ways acknowledge him, and he
will make your paths straight" (Prov. 3:5-6). We must live in the
constant reality that Christ is in our midst, waiting for us to ask
Him for wisdom and for direction. Jesus clearly said:

> Again, I tell you that if two of you on earth agree about
> anything you ask for, it will be done for you by my Father
> in heaven. For where two or three come together in my
> name, there am I with them (Matt. 18:19-20).

As we nurture and encourage our spiritual children to seek the Lord in all things, their decisions will reflect a growing wisdom and a deepening intimacy with Him.

No one is exempt from making decisions. Every person—whether it is in the home, church, workplace, school or community—must make decisions that affect other people. Husbands and wives are appointed by the Lord to give leadership to their families. Pastors and elders are appointed by God to give leadership to their local church. Spiritual parents are appointed to give stewardship to their spiritual sons or daughters. A student who is captain of the football team is a leader to his school's team. In some capacity, most of us are in some sort of leadership position and must know how to make wise biblical decisions.

When we learn how to take responsibility for biblical decision making, we begin to notice that it works in the home, in the church, in a youth group, in business and in any other place where decisions need to be made. God's desire is to place a blessing on spiritual fathers and mothers and on spiritual families as they follow His principles of leadership and of decision making.

God wants spiritual parents of all kinds to train those they mentor in biblical decision making so that they do not become autocratic leaders or live in fear of making decisions that affect others. When spiritual children learn to hear from their heavenly Father and honor their spiritual parents and others impacted by their decisions, they will make wise and godly decisions.

Key Questions for Practical Application

1. How do you believe decision making should be made within the church? Within the home?
2. What is servant leadership, and how does it apply to your life?
3. Briefly describe a time when you laid aside your plans because they did not coincide with what the rest of your family or team wanted.

12

Avoiding Pitfalls

Key: You must trust God and be
wise in all your relationships.

We are all held accountable in one way or another. In civil society,
there are laws to obey, and if we fail to obey them, we suffer the
consequences. In Christian society, likewise, there are guidelines
that govern relationships. Of special interest here are the guidelines that can help spiritual parents and their spiritual children
avoid relational problems.

Discuss Expectations

At the outset of any successful spiritual parenting relationship,
it is wise to discuss expectations. What are both persons in the
relationship looking for? Explain to your spiritual daughter or
son how you would like to help her or him and what you expect
from the one you mentor. Be honest and open. Invite your spiritual daughter or son to do the same. Goals and objectives for
the relationship should be discussed.

Then have your spiritual daughter or son assess her or
his current state. Ask questions to get the assessment started:
Are there already certain areas of life and ministry that you need
to grow in? Are there any major skeletons in your closet that
need to be dealt with immediately? What are your goals and the
kind of assistance you feel you need? Invite your spiritual child

to be vulnerable, and point out that you are not a mind reader. Oftentimes a relationship is held captive by secret, unmet expectations. I have done it with my wife and with those who have parented me. *Why not?* I have reasoned. *They should know. They know me and are older (or are wiser, have more experience or know the situation better than I do).*

Neither you nor your daughter or son should hold each other captive, play games or attempt manipulation. If your spiritual daughter or son desires prayer or a hug, tell her or him to feel free to initiate it! Invite the spiritual daughter or son to resist mental and emotional hi-jinks, which get a person nowhere but frustrated and self-consumed.

I once heard about a very angry son who persistently harassed his natural father for not being there for him after the parents divorced during his growing-up years. Nothing the father did could make up for all his shortcomings in his son's eyes. The father took his son's berating for some time and then in an unguarded moment blurted out, "Did you ever stop to think you were hardly a perfect son?" Why do we as sons expect perfection of our fathers and yet excuse our own imperfect and immature behaviors?

When you enter into a spiritual mentoring relationship, you accept your spiritual daughter or son for who she or he is. The two of you do not compete with each other. You do not have to be better than anyone (but being different is okay). Do not compare yourself to the other person. The end result of comparison is usually either a feeling of being devalued by (inadequacy) or being better than (pride) the one to whom you are comparing yourself—and neither feeling will deepen the relationship. Comparison will undermine any and all accomplishments. Remember, this is a give-and-take relationship. You are not out to change anyone; that is the Holy Spirit's work.

Decide on some practical times to get together. It is a good idea to determine how you can best maintain contact with each other—face-to-face, by phone, by email or by texting. Both of you should respect the other's time and responsibilities so that impositions are avoided.

Determine how often and for how long you will meet. One breakfast meeting each month may be adequate for some people to develop a healthy relationship, while new Christians or those in crisis may need more get-togethers (weekly or bi-weekly). These planned, regular contacts should be interlaced with a lot of spontaneous contact, and you should plan some meetings on the other's turf.

Discuss early on the length of the relationship: Some people may foresee the relationship lasting for a certain period of time while other people hope it will continue as a long-term relationship (of course, this needs to be re-evaluated periodically). A spiritual parent may maintain a close relationship for a lifetime with one spiritual child, but with other spiritual children he or she may be close for only a few years or even just a few months. Whether it is for a mutually agreed-upon time period or an ongoing commitment, it is the health of the relationship that is vital! Keep it healthy by periodically examining the friendship to determine if continuing is God's best plan.

Eventually, if the set goal has been achieved, both of you should take the responsibility for the winding down of the relationship. This does not mean that ties are broken and you never speak to each other again. In a natural family, when a son marries, he is still his father's son. The father may no longer have as much input in his life, but the son remains a son. In some natural relationships, a phone call now and then will be all it takes to maintain a father-son relationship. The same thing is true of a spiritual parenting relationship, though it is important that a spiritual child knows that the spiritual parent is available if needed, even if a regular and deep time together is in the past.

I have served in a spiritual fathering relationship with some Christian leaders for more than 25 years. Although they still look to me as a spiritual father, I now consider them to be my peers. This relational evolution should be the aim of all spiritual mentoring relationships; after all, the point is to grow up new spiritual parents and release them for God's glory!

Deal with Relational Problems

One Saturday morning years ago, my then six-year-old daughter Leticia begged me to make her some pancakes for breakfast. Her mother and sisters were gone for the morning, and she was stuck with me as the cook. My cooking skills being what they are, I pleaded with her, "Please, Leticia, couldn't you just eat cereal today?" She persisted, so I obliged.

Half asleep, I read the instructions incorrectly and the end product looked unfit for human consumption. I asked her again to please eat cereal instead. She again staunchly persisted.

This time the oil in the pan caught on fire! I knew it was not going to be a good day. (We later had to repaint the blackened spot the fire left on the ceiling.)

"Please try again, Daddy," Leticia implored, making good use of her big blue eyes. How could I resist? I decided just to ignore the instructions. This time, without following the recipe on the side of the box, I began to mix together milk and eggs and any other ingredients I could find that I thought might work. Amazingly enough, the concoction looked edible. With a prayer of thanks, I slid the golden pancakes onto a plate, drenched them in lots of syrup (which I did not, thankfully, have to make) and placed them in front of my ever-patient daughter.

Leticia took one bite of my freshly made pancakes, looked up at me with a mixture of despair and disappointment and said, "Daddy, may I have cereal, please?"

Today, I meet people throughout the Body of Christ who have given up on the spiritual parenting they long for because complicated and unpredictable situations arose in previous spiritual parenting relationships.

Sometimes spiritual parents—and spiritual children, too—find themselves in discordant relationships and quit. It's not that the spiritual parents or children did not try. Perhaps they misread the scriptural directions and the relationship flopped. Or maybe a spiritual child was parented by a spiritual parent who sought to control rather than encourage. Yet giving up entirely on all spiritual parenting relationships because some do not work out is like throwing the baby out with the bathwater (or like never eating pancakes again because of one little house fire).

I remember my son, Josh, playing with a model electric train as a kid, and time and time again the train would round one particular corner, fly off the track, and lay helpless on its side, spinning its wheels. It could not possibly get back on the tracks without outside help. It was only when I picked up the train and gently set it on the tracks that it could run again.

It is a fact that people have a tendency to get off track spiritually and relationally. But our Father God, if we allow Him, will pick us up when we get derailed and place us back on track. Only then can we arrive at the destination God intended for us. The Lord is a great Redeemer! He wants to heal our hurts, and He wants to help believers recover what Satan has tried to steal from them.

Every relationship experiences rough patches. Friction is unavoidable in spiritual mentoring, but following a few simple guidelines can keep the friction to a minimum and get us back on track when we derail.

Be Realistic about Meeting Needs

Because of the powerful connection between the individuals involved in a spiritual parenting relationship, there is a danger that you will take on too much responsibility for the growth of the spiritual child. If you do not guard against this kind of unhealthy dependence, a daughter or son may begin to demand more than you can or should give. Before you know it, the relationship becomes self-serving.

Tony Fitzgerald from Church of the Nations has served as a spiritual father to church leaders scattered across the globe for more than 20 years. He gave me this wise advice during one of our conversations: "Fathering is not to meet every need but to be sure every need is met."

In the story of the good Samaritan, the compassionate Samaritan attended to the wounded man's bruises, placed him on his donkey and took him to an inn. At that point, the Samaritan's job was finished. He entrusted the wounded man to the innkeeper and then left. He did not meet every need of the wounded man, but he made sure his every need was attended to. (If you want to read the story for yourself, see Luke 10:25-37.)

In the same way, you as a spiritual parent can meet certain needs of your spiritual daughter or son, but you will probably need to entrust your spiritual child to others to meet further needs of the child. For example, you may direct your son or daughter to helpful resources—books, CDs, videos, podcasts and other spiritual leaders and counselors—in order to help fill one of your child's needs without directly meeting the need yourself. You must be realistic about which needs you are able to and should meet, and then you should direct your spiritual daughter or son to other sources for the fulfillment of other needs.

Maintain Proper Emotional Boundaries

A relationship goes downhill when two people lean too much on each other rather than on the Lord. If your spiritual daughter or son looks to you to solve all problems or meet all needs, the relationship becomes need-driven and unhealthy.

Those involved in spiritual mothering relationships are especially vulnerable to becoming too dependent, because most women have a natural tendency to form close friendships. Because of this tendency, the spiritual mother and daughter may tend to absorb themselves too deeply in the spiritual relationship. If either party becomes possessive and demanding, an unhealthy dependency forms, and stronger boundaries need to be drawn and maintained.

"Dependent relationships become ingrown and create a seedbed for one person to become emotionally dependent on another,"[1] according to author and friend Steve Prokopchak. In his book *Recognizing Emotional Dependency,* he defines emotional dependency as "the condition resulting when the ongoing presence and/or nurturing of another is believed necessary for personal security."[2] Steve goes on to say:

It's true that we need others. I believe that relationship with God and with others is the most important thing in life. . . . However, our need for relationship cannot be allowed to become the center of a person's life. The emotionally dependent person feels as though he cannot exist or function without this relationship. Mistakenly, this association is an attempt to meet the need for intimacy and security.[3]

In spiritual fathering and mothering relationships, proper boundaries must be maintained in order to maintain healthy relationships. This means that both you and your spiritual son or daughter must be sure of your identities in Christ and want to please Him rather than any other person. Make sure your spiritual child understands the need to trust the Holy Spirit more than she or he trusts you.

Here are a few practical steps you can take to draw and maintain healthy relational boundaries:

1. *Talk about mutual expectations of the relationship.* As you build a friendship with your spiritual son or daughter, maintain a healthy sense of self. Otherwise, emotional dependency happens.
2. *Early on in the relationship, determine what you are and aren't responsible for in your spiritual daughter or son's life.* Ultimately, you are not the child's spiritual caretaker; Jesus is.
3. *Know where to draw the line in your time spent with your spiritual son or daughter.*
4. *Be trustworthy.* Don't betray confidential information your spiritual daughter or son tells you.
5. *Remember that spiritual parenting is an act of service.* Realize that the relationship is in place to encourage your spiritual child in her or his relationship with Christ.

Get Outside Help If Needed

Sometimes you will need help to solve a severe problem in your spiritual daughter or son's life. There is no need to be alarmed by such a situation; a person making progress on a spiritual journey is often beset by sins that need to be dealt with. Stubborn struggles may include depression; addiction to sex, alcohol or drugs; or a problem dealing with anger appropriately. (An excellent source of information about counseling is Steve Prokopchak's manual called *Counseling Basics,* a guidebook intended to help lay leaders counsel those they are mentoring.[4])

If your spiritual son or daughter has a severe ongoing addiction or emotional problem that you are not able to deal with, he or she may benefit from meeting with a professional counselor. You can stay involved in the spiritual child's life and at the same time have the additional support available to help the son or daughter through the difficult times. (Your church may have a list of recommended Christian counselors, or a list of therapists in your area can be found at www.aacc.net, the website of the American Association of Christian Counselors.)

End Well If the Relationship Must End

Although it is usually possible to sort out problems without dissolving the spiritual parenting relationship, sometimes there may be negative interpersonal dynamics that make the relationship impossible to continue. Keep in mind, though, that if a once-beneficial relationship becomes critical and disappointment sets in, you should not immediately bolt from the scene!

Address the root of the conflict before it causes irrevocable damage. Be vulnerable and candid in your communication, and pray together. Try to resolve the conflict as painlessly as possible. It may be helpful to have a trusted third party guide your spiritual parenting relationship through the conflict.

If the problem cannot be resolved, remember that a spiritual fathering or mothering relationship is not a covenant bond; it is a spiritual impartation into the life of another that allows freedom and flexibility. If the time comes for a separation, the love relationship you have with Christ and each other will help you to discern how to graciously and lovingly bow out of the relationship. Allow the Lord to be your comfort so that you do not grow bitter or refuse to take the risk of another spiritual parenting relationship.

Above all, be supportive. As a spiritual parent, you have the heart of a natural mother or father. Your greatest aspiration is to provide a supportive environment to help your daughter or son discover what God has for her or him and then assist the child in finding her or his own answer. Lest you forget, spiritual fathers and mothers are never substitutes for the Holy Spirit. Supporting, rather than advising, honors the uniqueness of the spiritual child's own calling. Be a spiritual parent who helps your son or daughter fully live out God's calling and vision for his or her life.

Ministering in Your Fields

I live in the fertile agricultural area of Lancaster County, Pennsylvania. Its lush green and golden fields of corn, alfalfa, barley and wheat cover the landscape. Whenever I fly over the area, I am amazed at all the shapes and sizes the fields display, with their unique colors and easily recognizable boundaries. Each field represents a particular crop waiting to be harvested. This diversity of crops gives our community the distinction of producing more agricultural products and yielding more food than any other non-irrigated county in our nation.

Similar to the diversity of fields of crops in my county are the fields of ministry that the Lord has assigned to each person. These ministry fields that dot the landscape of our lives are our spheres of influence, responsibility and anointing. These spiritual fields give us great opportunities to experience God's blessing and empowerment, as long as we work within the boundaries of our fields: "We, however, will not boast beyond proper limits, but will confine our boasting to the field God has assigned to us, a field that reaches even to you" (2 Cor. 10:13). The Greek word that is translated "field" in 2 Corinthians 10 is *metron*, which is defined as a measure of activity that defines the limits of one's power and influence.

Every person has several different areas that they have the power to influence and make decisions about. A married person has a field of ministry with a spouse. If the couple has children, they have another field that extends to their family. If an individual leads a small group, he or she has another sphere of influence that includes the spiritual responsibility for the small-group members. An involvement in a church is another sphere in which to experience God's blessing, while communities are yet another. As a member of a neighborhood, each person has a field of ministry on his or her street as neighbors are served and prayers for them to come to Christ are offered. The workplace provides an additional sphere of influence. Spiritual parents, likewise, have fields of ministry with their spiritual daughters and sons: they have opportunities to influence, bless and strengthen their spiritual children's lives.

When I was a farmer, I did not have the option of taking my tractor over to plow my neighbor's field and then deciding which crops he would plant. That was up to him—it was his field! I also never contemplated going into his field to plant my seed; this would have been counterproductive, because I did not own that field and could never claim the harvest from it. I planted, cultivated and harvested crops that fell within my own property lines. A person who wants to have prosperous fields of ministry understands that each of his or her fields has certain limitations and boundaries, just as the alfalfa farmer knows that if he or she wants the best possible yield for his or her crop, the farmer's alfalfa must be kept from crossing over into the neighbor farmer's corn. These boundaries give protection to the field and must be carefully and prayerfully respected.

Similarly, where I live, farmers often post at the edges of their fields several *No Trespassing* signs meant to deter hunters from tramping across their fields during hunting season. In life, there are often disastrous results when someone trespasses on another's field. You have only to look at today's divorce statistics to see the trail of devastation left when a married person steps across his or her marriage boundaries into someone else's field, be it owned by a single person or another married couple. As a parent, you have authority and responsibility for your own family's field. You cannot tell your neighbors how to raise their children because you do not have authority in their home. A mother-in-law gets the stereotypical reputation of an interfering, meddlesome creature who disrupts her child's marriage only when she moves beyond her area of authority and infringes the boundaries of the marriage relationship that belongs to her child.

The Boundaries of Your Fields

Like the fields of our farming county, which are clearly distinguished by shape and color and by boundaries such as roads and fences, your ministry field as a spiritual parent has boundaries. As a spiritual parent, you must have a clear understanding of the margins of your field. You should never presume to speak into another's life unless that person has opened her or his borders to you. In other words, you cannot intrude into the life of another until a relationship of trust has been built that opens the door for you to speak candidly.

Of course, if a spiritual daughter or son under your care clearly has sin in her or his life, you must lovingly appeal to her or to him:

> If your brother sins against you, go and show him his fault, just between the two of you. If he listens to you, you have won your brother over. But if he will not listen, take one or two others along, so that "every matter may be established by the testimony of two or three witnesses." If he refuses to listen to them, tell it to the church; and if he refuses to listen even to the church, treat him as you would a pagan or a tax collector (Matt. 18:15-17).

Even when you thus confront the spiritual child, however, you must be careful to allow your child to take responsibility for his or her own boundaries and personal choices. Every spiritual child must learn to live with the consequences of decisions made; your place is to encourage and exhort, not to dictate or control.

Just as in all relationships, spiritual parenting should come with some agreed-upon boundaries from the start of the relationship. If time restraints and needs are not thoroughly discussed at the outset, the son or daughter may want too much of your time or need too much help on issues that are outside your field. For example, expecting from a spiritual father or mother things like a personal loan or free babysitting for the kids every Saturday may go well beyond what is appropriate for the boundaries of the relationship.

Conversely, it is also possible for spiritual parents to overstep their boundaries and exhibit unhealthy control. This can happen even in prayer. For example, if a spiritual mother or father prays that her or his spiritual child would approach a certain issue exactly as the parent does ("because such-and-such is the answer for everyone"), then that parent is attempting to change the child rather than allowing God to speak to the child's heart. This kind of control breaches the boundaries and is a type of spiritual witchcraft, because it is actually praying with the intent to control rather than praying for God's plan. True spiritual parents, with their maturity and experience, help their daughters and sons discern what God is saying to them inside the boundaries of their own fields of responsibility.

God gave the apostles Paul and Peter different fields and boundaries: Paul's call and anointing was to reach the Gentiles, while Peter's call and anointing was to reach the Jews (see Acts 17–21). These lines were so clearly drawn that Paul confronted Peter when the other apostle crossed over into his field (see Gal. 2:11-13). In Antioch Peter temporarily helped Paul, but because Peter still carried with him the old notion that Gentiles could not be accepted without circumcision, he allowed his human prejudice toward the uncircumcised Gentiles to undermine what God was doing in that city. Paul rebuked Peter for his infringement, because he knew that God had given him authority to reach the Gentiles. Peter was interfering in his field.

Later in the Scriptures, we learn that Peter readjusted his thinking on the circumcision matter. He is recorded as speaking favorably of Paul's work (see Acts 15:7-11). God had to expand Peter's thinking, because his field of ministry was so closely focused on the Jews. He learned, not only to avoid infringing on the ministry fields of others, but also to submit when he was in their fields.

We see many examples of this kind of submission throughout the New Testament. Although Paul gave clear oversight to
those in his field, when he came to Jerusalem he submitted to
James, the lead apostle in the city. Paul knew he had crossed the
boundary into James's field (see Acts 15), and he clearly understood the need to come under the leader whom God had granted
authority in the field he was now in. When fields of ministry
coexist in this way, with everyone respecting each other's boundaries, there is unity and respect for each other.

Authority in Your Fields

You have the authority to speak into your spiritual child's life if
you clearly understand your boundaries. The apostle Paul understood his sphere of influence and reminded the Corinthians
that he only operated in the sphere in which God had appointed
him. He did not go around troubling churches founded by others; he only boasted of the Corinthian church because he was
responsible to the Lord for them:

> We, however, will not boast beyond measure, but with-
> in the limits of the sphere which God appointed us—a
> sphere which especially includes you. For we are not ex-
> tending ourselves beyond our sphere (thus not reaching
> you), for it was to you that we came with the gospel of
> Christ; not boasting of things beyond measure, that is,
> in other men's labors, but having hope, that as your faith
> is increased, we shall be greatly enlarged by you in our
> sphere (2 Cor. 10:13-15, *NKJV*).

Paul was careful not to take the credit or responsibility for another person's field of ministry. He knew his own sphere's shape,
color and boundary fences; and he operated within God's authority and anointing for its oversight.

Likewise, you have authority to speak into the life of your
spiritual daughter or son because you have taken on the responsibility for the spiritual growth of that child, and the child has giv-
en to you the freedom to do so. In general, you have permission

to speak into your spiritual child's life when the spiritual child places her- or himself within your boundaries. When you earn that privilege through getting to know your child and listening to the child, you gain the authority to give advice. Nevertheless, it must be done carefully and wisely.

In the mid-1970s, a phenomenon called the discipleship (or shepherding) movement became somewhat popular. Good discipleship principles were sometimes overshadowed by unhealthy one-on-one relationships in which leaders required those under their authority to get approval before their spiritual children made decisions about such issues as dating, marriage and even visiting relatives during holidays. Occasionally, believers moved halfway across the country to follow their spiritual leaders to a new location, and in some cases, lives were turned upside down and families split apart. This movement led to unbiblical obedience to human leaders. Some of these leaders twisted the biblical principles of authority and accountability by stepping into fields they did not own and attempting to make decisions that were not rightfully theirs to make.

Absolute control is unhealthy, and many individuals in the discipleship movement found themselves in what might be called unholy covenants. While a holy covenant is a promise ordained and sealed by God, an unholy covenant is made with a person or group that thinks it is above and beyond the Holy Spirit's leading. You as a spiritual parent must not make decisions for your spiritual child or ask your child to make unholy covenants. You must never seek to control the one you mentor or to promote dependency in any way.

In a spiritual parenting relationship, if the Lord calls either the parent or the child to serve elsewhere—to serve in another field—the individual so called should be released to go. Helping others to find their places of most fruitful ministry is a biblical mandate. James 4:13-15 tells us to always remain open to God's leading in our lives: "You who say, 'Today or tomorrow we will go to this or that city.' . . . Instead, you ought to say, 'If it is the Lord's will, we will live and do this or that.'" A spiritual parent must allow his or her spiritual child the freedom to go, if and when God calls the child elsewhere; and a spiritual child must allow his or her spiritual parent the freedom to go also. No one ever has authority to override God's direction.

Grace for Your Fields

Along with the authority you as a spiritual parent are granted within the boundaries of your field, a portion of grace is given to do the job. Grace is often described as the free unmerited favor of God on the undeserving and ill-deserving, but it also can be defined as the desire and the power to do God's will. Grace is a divine energy that the Holy Spirit releases in your life to help you victoriously accomplish tasks within your field of ministry.

How do I know that God gives you grace to operate within your field of ministry? The word *metron*, which we saw earlier in 2 Corinthians 10:13, has a slightly different meaning in Ephesians 4:7: "But to each one of us grace has been given as Christ apportioned it." Here the word "apportioned" is a translation of the same word "metron." It follows that for each metron, or field of ministry, Christ apportions special grace.

Because we all have different-sized fields, God apportions grace in varying amounts according to our needs. Through the Spirit's leading, spiritual fathers and mothers will know how many spiritual children they can parent at a time, and they will receive grace to spiritually parent them all well. On the other hand, if spiritual parents step out of the fields of ministry to which they are assigned, they step out of God's grace—and that is not a good place to be! Good spiritual fathers and mothers remain in their fields of ministry and thus remain in the grace of God, and they caution their spiritual children to do the same.

The Fruit of Your Fields

When you cultivate your fields within their boundaries and receive God's grace for your ministries, your fields will yield fruit. You will rejoice with the psalmist: "LORD, you have assigned me my portion and my cup; you have made my lot secure. The boundary lines have fallen for me in pleasant places; surely I have a delightful inheritance" (Ps. 16:5-6).

Rather than limit you, boundary lines allow you to be fruitful in your spheres of influence. The fields to which God assigns you are protected, secure places of growth. You can flourish as you learn how to receive your inheritance (remember that your inheritance is your spiritual children!) within those fields. Within the boundaries of your fields, you receive rich blessings, because you are where the Lord wants you to be, and you know when you are in the right spiritual parenting relationship(s) because each relationship yields fruit! Your children mature in their relationships with the Lord and are released to parent the next generation of spiritual children.

I was speaking at a leadership conference a few years ago and joined the group of about 500 pastors and Christian leaders in the audience for an evening service. The moderator of the conference asked a friend of mine with whom I had spoken earlier in the conference to stand. My friend had served as a pastor in various states over the years and at that time pastored a church of about 50 people in Dallas, Texas. After he stood, the moderator asked every man who had been a spiritual son or had been influenced by this pastor to stand: Men stood up all over the auditorium! I was deeply moved. This man had learned to obey God as a spiritual parent and to release his spiritual children to start their own ministries—and the result was a very fruitful field!

The Development of Your Fields

Growing as a Christian demands that you grow in your personality, calling, unique abilities and spiritual giftedness and that you help your spiritual son or daughter develop the right tools and guide him or her in the same process. Understanding these areas and tending them toward growth will help you and your child become all God intends you and your child to be. As the spiritual parent, you come alongside a child to encourage and give that little push out of the nest so that your spiritual child can learn to fly on his or her own. Of course, it is the Lord who determines and expands the fields; He is the One who opens the doors to the fields that are just right for each person (see Ps. 75:6-7).

Remember that as a spiritual parent, you should seek to develop your own fields to their fullest, being faithful with the grace God has given. Timing is everything in developing your fields of ministry. Ecclesiastes 8:5-6 indicates that there is a proper time, place and method for everything. David is the classic example of this precept in action: He was called and anointed to be king, but there already was a reigning king. David, though his calling was clear, did not seize power or attempt to overthrow the existing authority. Instead, he allowed God to promote him at the proper time (see Ps. 78:70-72). He waited in faith and grew into the king God had anointed him to be.

If you are responsible within your present fields and develop them well, God will enhance them. Allow God to promote you. Sometimes when I teach this concept, it sounds like a business principle. It is true that many successful businesses have adopted this Kingdom principle of promoting those who are faithful in the areas that have been assigned to them. But this was in the Bible long before modern business owners recognized it as an effective management method. Whether you are called to be a spiritual parent to someone, called to start a small group or called to plant a new church, remember: Timing is up to God. In addition, help your spiritual son or daughter determine his or her fields and encourage the one you mentor to wait to be promoted by the Lord when change is on the horizon. A spiritual child may not have the maturity to see this, and your wise guidance in this area is one way you can protect him or her from mistakes and disappointment.

In God's timing, He will expand your fields and the fields of your spiritual child. Your job in the meantime is to tend and harvest the fruit that is growing now.

Responsibility for Your Fields

Paul had a sense of responsibility for his spiritual children in the Corinthian church (see 2 Cor. 11:28-29). You too must be responsible and, as a spiritual mother or father, stand in the gap to intercede for your spiritual child. Ezekiel 22:30 clearly pictures prayer warfare as a believer standing in the gap between God's mercy and humanity's need. God has given you, the spiritual parent, the authority to intercede in this way.

As a spiritual parent, you must take possession of your inheritance by interceding diligently. Intercession restricts and destroys satanic strongholds and evil forces of the enemy and allows the Holy Spirit to bring godly influences into your life as well as that of your spiritual son or daughter. You are given responsibility and oversight for multiple fields of ministry: your home, church, business, community and spiritual children. These are your fields of assignment from the Lord. It is your responsibility to tend and develop them, whether large or small. As a spiritual father or mother, rise up in faith and possess the fields the Lord has given you!

Take possession of your fields by working faithfully in His grace and respecting others' fields around you. Christ has entrusted your fields to you. Walk in His grace and produce a diversity of crops in carefully cultivated fields. You will yield more healthy fruit than you could ever imagine!

Key Questions for Practical Application

1. What is wrong with comparing yourself to others?
2. How are encouraging and exhorting different from dictating and controlling?
3. What are the blessings of maintaining your own fields, and what are the pitfalls of overstepping boundaries?

13

Releasing Your Spiritual Children

Key: When the time is right, you need to let your spiritual daughters and sons fly!

In his book *Disciple*, minister and teacher Dr. Juan Carlos Ortiz writes that leaders must know how to release their people so that they can grow spiritually:

> But you know what happens in the modern church? We pastors stop somewhere along the way; we know how . . . to administrate, to help, to have some healings, or even to teach—but then we stop moving. We become corks. The sheep grow and grow and start jamming up behind us, unable to grow further until we grow some more ourselves. They keep listening to our sermons, and soon they know everything we know, and then we have nothing but a pressure chamber.
>
> The pastor is not a cork intentionally; . . . he is a victim of the structure like everyone else. It's always been done that way.
>
> If the pressure becomes great enough, the pastor gets uncomfortable enough to ask the bishop for a transfer. So the bishop takes out one cork and replaces him with another!

If it is a congregational denomination that doesn't have bishops, the problem is even worse. The pressure keeps building until the channel finally explodes and the cork flies out! He gets really banged up in the explosion, of course, sometimes so badly that he can no longer continue in the ministry.

All this is avoided, of course, if the pastor keeps on growing to apostleship and the sheep keep growing right behind him.

If a pastor is truly a father to his congregation, he cannot be changed (or exploded) every two or three years. What family changes fathers every two years? Maybe our churches are more like clubs that elect presidents for a certain term and then elect someone else. But if we are family, we are a family; we stay together. The father keeps turning over responsibility to his sons [and daughters] as they grow.[1]

Only a dysfunctional parent keeps his or her grown children at home when the children are ready to marry and build homes of their own; a normal parent encourages his or her children to go and establish their own homes! In the same way, any spiritual leader who keeps those under his or her care from becoming all the Lord has called them to be is dysfunctional. Such a pastor is not functioning as a proper leader. Sadly, there are many in the Church who are stunted, immature and impotent due to "leadership" of this kind.

When our son, Josh, was 15, he was responsible to mow the lawn each week (but this is not why the Lord gave him to us!). Mowing our lawn trained him and gave him the skills and motivation to mow his own lawn in the future. In the same way, we train our spiritual children with knowledge and passion so that they will do likewise for the next generation.

If spiritual blessings are not passed on to our spiritual children, the next generation is in danger of losing everything. When God's people took possession of the Promised Land, they served the Lord as long as the leaders set good examples for them and gave them godly instructions. But when Joshua and the elders of that generation died, the children of Israel forgot the mercies of God to Israel: "When all that generation had been gathered to their fathers, another generation arose after them who did not know the Lord nor the work which He had done for Israel" (Judg. 2:10, NKJV).

Apparently, Joshua and the elders had not trained others to inherit and then pass on a continuing spiritual legacy. Without spiritual fathers to remind them of what the Lord had done for them when He brought them out of Canaan, the people turned away from God. They no longer remembered or cared about the nation's covenant to obey the Law of the Lord. A spiritual legacy was lost to the next generation because no one had trained them to train others, which is the essence of spiritual parenting.

After Jesus rose from the dead and just before He ascended into heaven, He encouraged the Twelve to take on the responsibility of His Church. Jesus set an example for us to release our spiritual children to "go and do it" (for a discussion of the model Jesus set for us, see chapter 9). We need not be afraid of this step! When Jesus sent out the 72, He exclaimed when they returned, "I saw Satan fall like lightning from heaven" (Luke 10:18). Jesus witnessed His ministry, multiplied by 72, confounding the work of the enemy. And lest we forget, Jesus promised that we would do greater works than He had done (see John 14:12).

What are the greater works? We can only find out if we follow His example and release our spiritual children to multiply our ministries.

Release Them to Reproduce

Once while I was teaching a leadership-training seminar in Honolulu, Hawaii, I met a young man who had been sent out by his church a year before to plant a new church in neighboring Pearl City. This church plant had reached many young people with the gospel—70 young people had given their lives to Christ within the past few weeks! I wanted to experience this dynamic ministry for myself, so the young pastor agreed to take me to a youth meeting before he dropped me off at the airport.

We jumped into his station wagon and headed for the local school where the meeting was held. Inside, the young people were singing wholeheartedly, worshiping the Lord with their arms outstretched. They meant business with God! After a time of worship, everyone sat down and the lights flicked on. The youth pastor grabbed the microphone. "Everyone needs to be in a power huddle," he charged the group of new believers. "It's a place where you can get to know other kids, and there are people to help you out when you have a problem or a question about your life with God."

After the meeting, the pastor explained the truth they had discovered. "We have so far reached 225 young people, mostly from unsaved homes, and we've found that these kids need relationships. So we started power huddles—small groups for young people. The young people in power huddles are growing in God, while the young people who are not involved are having a hard time."

With the heart of a spiritual parent, the pastor revealed his releasing strategy: "I've told our youth pastor that he must plant a new church with these young people when he believes the time is right. I had to tell the church about the strategy, or I might be tempted to keep him here in order to help me build this church."

This pastor had learned the value of reaching the next generation and empowering them to reproduce themselves. There is among us a whole new generation of pastors, small-group leaders and church planters who are enthusiastic and often unconventional. Though we parents may not always understand our children, we must always encourage them to dream big and allow God to use us to help them fulfill those dreams.

If you are a pastor or a Christian leader, let me take a moment and address a few remarks specifically to you. You must commission this next generation to establish their own power huddles and their own new churches. You must not hold them back. Empower these young people and then rejoice with them when they reproduce!

The younger generation in our churches wants to experience something new and relevant to their age group. Believers in the 18-to-35 age bracket have shared with me that although they are involved in their churches and respect and honor their leaders, they believe God is calling them to something new. They are no longer satisfied with traditional church structures. They come into the Kingdom looking for reality, not religious structures. They want relationships, not outdated church programs. They have a God-given desire to build new homes.

I understand completely. I remember how I felt when I was in my 20s and the Lord called me to start a new church—a new wine-skin—just as He did with many of my generation. But new wine-skins eventually get old, and members of my generation are now the parents. God has given the younger generation the same burden to birth new wineskins, with a different vision for a different era. As spiritual parents, it is in our best interests to parent them and then release them to build their own homes and reproduce.

During the past few years, I have been privileged to disciple a team of young leaders who have started a new type of church in our community: house churches, or as some call them, micro-churches. Many of them do not normally meet on Sundays but during the week instead. Most of them eat a meal at every meeting. Instead of building buildings, they plan to start more small churches. They are burdened to meet the needs of the poor of our community. They meet in homes weekly and all together at various times throughout the year. It is a new church for a new generation.

When I was in my 20s, the new church did not look at all like the church of the generation before me. So why should I expect the church of the next generation to look like mine? I have chosen to release the next generation and help them build new wineskins that meet the needs of their generation. My role is to be a father, to support them in their dreams from God.[2]

Release Them for the Harvest

In 1996, my friend Jim Pesce started a new church, Harvest Family Community Church, in Keswick, Ontario. Jim and his wife, Deb,

were committed to practicing the principles of spiritual fathering and mothering. More than 84 percent of their church mem-
bership were new believers who came to Christ since their church
was formed. Jim and Deb have now turned the church leadership
over to their spiritual sons and daughters, the spiritual children
they parented when the church began. Jim's personal insights
are a vivid picture of the harvest being reaped for the Lord that
began with Jim and Deb sowing into the lives of just a few:

> At the start of our new church, Deb and I spent most of
> our time with about six newly saved couples. We not only
> ministered as a team but chose to spend free time togeth-
> er having fun. This is important. Most new Christians
> need more care and support than instruction.
>
> The ones we brought to Christ have our "spiritual
> DNA"; they share our vision and our hearts and have
> our full trust. Because we are like family, there is much
> room for acceptance, correction and patience to cover
> the many offenses we cause one another. They know that
> we will be with them over the long haul and accept them
> with all their flaws and sins. We love them for who they
> are, not for what they can accomplish for us.
>
> We believe in them! By spending time with oth-
> ers, they "catch our spirit" and multiply the ministry.
> Our passions become theirs as they walk with us in
> ministry situations.
>
> The greatest struggle we face in [spiritual parenting]
> is choosing to say no to the many other demanding voic-
> es that would keep us from choosing to spend quality
> time with those special few we are [spiritually parenting].
> Busyness is the destroyer of spiritual parenting.

Just as the church name indicates, Harvest Family Community
Church is a spiritual family that consists of spiritual parents
and children. They have discovered that every believer is called
to parent as that adult grows to spiritual maturity. This church
is now touching the nations of the world.

Omar and Pat Beiler, who are missionaries with the Assemblies of God, served for many years in Austria. They grew an existing church in Vienna by discipling several young people from the university, and the small Bible study group expanded as the Beilers became spiritual parents to the young believers. Four years after starting the small-group ministry, they invited me to conduct a training seminar for them. I was amazed! They had 400 people attending 36 small spiritual family groups scattered throughout their city. Seventy-five young leaders attended the seminar, each of whom was already producing spiritual children of his or her own. This church, with its focus on spiritual parenting, had become the largest multi-cultural church in Austria's history since the days of the Reformation—all within four years!

This past week I was in Kisumu, Kenya, with my friends Hesbone and Violet Odindo. Just over six years ago, Hesbone traveled from the city of Nairobi where they lived to the Kisumu region of his village, Kadawa Village. There he led a few persons to Christ. He and Violet then moved back to this village and became spiritual parents to these new believers and started a cell group with them in the home of a relative. Today, this small cell group has multiplied into nine new churches, dozens of cell groups made up of 2,000 people. All of this was built on relational Christianity, as they trained a host of their spiritual children to become spiritual parents themselves—who in turn have trained another generation of spiritual parents. And the legacy continues on.

I believe the Lord is preparing to pour out His Spirit and bring revival to the Church in these last days. There will be a greater awakening to the things of God in our communities, and uncountable multitudes will be drawn into the kingdom of God. When the Lord pours out this new wine, we must have the new wineskins prepared or we will lose the harvest.

Down through history, there have been those who duplicated the Early Church's method of meeting house to house with positive results. John Wesley, the founder of the Methodist church, was one such individual. During the eighteenth century, he set up thousands of "class meetings" in which people met in homes to grow in God. He once made the comment that "more has happened in people's lives in close fellowship than in ten years of public preaching." More recently, in the twentieth century, David Yonggi Cho from Korea followed the New Testament Church's example of small groups and for many years has pastored the world's largest congregation.

I believe our Lord's strategy to prepare for the harvest is still the same: He wants to draw together common, ordinary believers who have encountered an extraordinary God, and He wants these believers to become spiritual families who will meet from house to house to disciple and train others, preparing for the harvest.

Many Christians today are thirsty for a great influx of new wine: new believers pouring into His kingdom. God is placing a desire within spiritual mothers and fathers to welcome these believers into the Kingdom and train them as spiritual daughters and sons and then release them to reap a harvest. When a young man and woman come together at the altar to be married, there is an expectation that they will eventually have children. The same principle applies to spiritual families. When people are in love with Jesus and with each other, spiritual children are the result. If we are to bring in the harvest God intends, we must make sure that our spiritual children grow up and reproduce spiritual children of their own, who in turn will grow more spiritual parents.

Key Questions for Practical Application

1. What type of leadership causes dysfunctional growth?
2. How can a spiritual legacy be lost?
3. How does busyness interfere with spiritual parenting, and what can you do about it?

14

Answering Your Call to Spiritual Parenthood

Key: God has called you,
so what are you waiting for?

Being a spiritual mom or dad is not a duty; it is a privilege. Did you ever notice how many times Paul the apostle opened his letters with an expression of gratitude for those he fathered in the Lord? For example, his epistle to Titus greeted the younger man as "my true son in our common faith" (Titus 1:4). Paul saw people as gifts from the Lord to cherish and encourage. They were not a burden but a reason to rejoice.

Total dependence on the Lord is a prerequisite for spiritual parenting. Psalm 127:1 says that "unless the LORD builds the house, its builders labor in vain." Unless we know we are called and unless we depend fully on the Lord to guide us as spiritual parents, our work and efforts are in vain. It is God who builds the lives of our spiritual children. We are only tools in His hands.

This psalm goes on to say that "sons are a heritage from the LORD,... born in one's youth" (vv. 3-4). I believe this means that we can start early! We don't have to wait until we have it "all together" to train spiritual children. No one is ever completely prepared to be a parent; we learn along the way.

Doing Away with Obstacles

Think about your own life. What are some of the things that hinder you from becoming a spiritual parent? If you find yourself hindered by one of the obstacles discussed below, don't sit passively by. Take a step of faith to learn what you need to know or to be healed from hurts in your past. Your spiritual children are waiting for your care.

Ignorance

A simple lack of knowledge keeps many from becoming spiritual parents today: Many dedicated Christian believers either have never heard of spiritual parenting or do not understand the concept. Paul told the people at Athens that God overlooks ignorance, but when the truth is made known, people need to repent and change their ways: "In the past God overlooked such ignorance, but now he commands all people everywhere to repent" (Acts 17:30). Today's Church must wake up to the need for spiritual fathering and mothering. When we understand that God is a God of families and that He wants each person to be a spiritual dad or mom to another person(s), we understand spiritual parenting; we are no longer ignorant and are responsible to respond!

I was ministering at a church in Hawaii, teaching on the truths of spiritual parenting and small-group ministry, when a young lawyer came to me after the meeting. He said enthusiastically, "I want to be a spiritual father. It all makes sense. I can do that! I can be a spiritual father to a small group of people who want to grow in God." I encouraged him to speak to his pastor about his desire to serve in this way. I later spoke to the lawyer's pastor and told him of the young man's enthusiasm.

With a big smile the pastor said, "I've been trying to get him to take leadership of a small group for a long time!" At last, the young man had his spiritual eyes opened to spiritual parenting. He had received a revelation of spiritual mentoring from the Lord and was responsible to act on it.

> Jesus asked His disciples, "Who do people say I am?" Peter replied, "You are the Christ, the Son of the living God." Jesus blessed Peter and told him, "Flesh and blood has not revealed this to you, but My Father who is in heaven" (see Matt. 16:13-17, *NKJV*).

In the same way that Peter received a revelation from the Father in heaven, we too each need a revelation from the Lord regarding spiritual parenting. If our eyes are not opened by the Father, we may be tempted to start yet another church program. That young Hawaiian lawyer saw clearly that he did not have to start a program—he simply needed to become a dad. He had faith in his heart that could accomplish it, being aware that dads learn by trial and error as they have kids of their own and look to the wisdom of their own parents. The young lawyer's pastor became both a spiritual father and a friend to him, reminding the younger man that he did not have to be perfect—he would learn along the way. The new spiritual father learned the truth about parenting, repented of his previous ignorance and responded to the need.

Ignorance may also come from a lack of modeling. The absence of a spiritual father or mother in your own life may cause you to sit on the sidelines, because you have no idea how to parent. Perhaps you never had a natural parent or a spiritual parent to guide you, and you now believe that without a father or mother figure in your own life you can never be a parent to someone else.

I recently read *Raising a Modern-Day Knight: A Father's Role in Guiding His Son to Authentic Manhood*. The author, Robert Lewis, tells how he grew up with a dad who was drunk much of the time. He had a father positionally, but emotionally his father was not involved in his life. Yet the author refused to allow his painful childhood to be an excuse not to be a good father to his own children. When he came to Christ and later had children of his own, he made a commitment to train a whole new generation of fathers to train their sons for God. Today, as a writer and pastor, he uses his platform to explain how the curse of a dysfunctional family can be broken when a person comes to Christ and walks in freedom. Like this example of a deprived son turned generous father, you must press on by faith and overcome. You *can* demonstrate a better way to your children.

You must not allow your perceptions to be distorted or your future to be determined by poorly modeled examples. Remember,

God is a perfect Father! He is the model of a Father who loves you perfectly and believes the best about you. No matter what you have experienced, you are accepted and loved by your heavenly Father.

Apathy

Indifference is another reason for some believers to avoid becoming a spiritual parent. As Christians we can get so caught up in making a living, taking our kids to soccer games and participating in civic organizations that it seems as if there is no time to be spiritual parents. But I challenge you to see these everyday activities as opportunities to develop spiritual relationships. You already have common interests with the other parents who are sitting in the stands and watching their children play sports. You're already cheering for the same team, sharing your children's achievements and disappointments.

Todd and Marie are parents who admit that it is hard balancing busy schedules that are filled with sports activities. They spend hours watching their children play baseball, soccer, basketball, football and swim. Over the years, they have developed close friendships with other parents and have invited several non-Christian families into their home, where they believe many spiritual seeds have been planted. As children continue to grow and participate in different activities, however, many parents lose contact with each other. That happened to Todd and Marie. When their son Seth was diagnosed with cancer, he could no longer participate in baseball, and they drifted apart from the other parents. However, the friendship with one family was quickly revived when that family's son was also diagnosed with cancer:

> Our [Todd and Marie's] family ended up in their family room praying over their son, and we continue to support them with prayer. Our relationship started back in Little League baseball, but now we have connected on a much deeper level. No matter where we are, we have opportunities to mentor someone else. Our relationships with others might not always be titled "spiritual parenting" but may seem to be more like natural friendships. But as we

keep our eyes focused on Jesus and seek to keep sports in the proper order, our spiritual eyes stay open to opportunities to minister.

When people are wrapped up in their own lives and selfish desires, they become apathetic to the things of God. Revelation 3:19 tells us clearly to "turn [repent] from your indifference and become enthusiastic about the things of God" (*TLB*).

Forty-five years ago, Floyd McClung and his wife, Sally, made a decision to disciple people. He said, "Not just bless them, or love them or build relationships with them but disciple them."

The McClungs have witnessed abundant fruit from their labors. For example, 38 churches grew out of one small group of leaders they discipled. One woman whom they discipled started a Bible study with prostitutes in the Red Light District in Amsterdam. Her Bible study grew into a church with more than 1,000 people who in turn planted numerous other churches.

The McClungs' amazing results from discipleship were not without personal sacrifices. Floyd said, "Our commitment to make disciples meant saying no to many other attractive opportunities and invitations. We are convinced after 45 years of ministry that it is the most crucial ministry decision we ever made."

Perseverance and faithfulness are prerequisites for spiritual parenting. As you repent of apathy and indifference, the Lord will give you grace and wisdom to take others with you as you go about your other activities. Jesus called His disciples first and foremost to *be with* Him. Your spiritual child will learn much more by watching you live your life than by listening to your sermons. It is easier than you think to accommodate others into your daily activities. Whether you're going to play golf or you're going shopping, take your spiritual child along. I often invite my spiritual sons with me on ministry trips. I value the time I get with various spiritual sons who join me on trips around the world.

Insecurity

Insecurity may tempt a person to think, *How could God ever use me? I don't know how to be a spiritual parent. I'm afraid. I don't know the Bible well enough. I need to get my life more together.* If you feel this way, you have a lot of company.

Moses told the Lord he could not speak properly (see Exod. 4:10). Jeremiah told the Lord he was too young (see Jer.1:6). Joshua was scared, and the Lord kept reassuring him that He would be with him just as He was with his "father" Moses (see Josh. 1:5). Gideon thought he was brought up in the wrong family for the Lord to use him (see Judg. 6:18). The list goes on and on.

Even the apostle Paul admitted to the Corinthian church that he had a deep sense of his own weakness that caused him to feel fearful and inadequate: "When I came to you, brothers, I did not come with eloquence or superior wisdom as I proclaimed to you the testimony about God. . . . I came to you in weakness and fear, and with much trembling" (1 Cor. 2:1-3). Nevertheless, Paul went on to declare that although his speech was not persuasive, the Holy Spirit's power was in his words (see 1 Cor. 2:4). He said it another way in 2 Timothy 1:7: "God did not give us a spirit of timidity, but a spirit of power, of love and of self-discipline."

Maybe you didn't go to seminary or Bible school, but the little you know is certainly more than the spiritual baby in Christ whom the Lord longs for you to parent. Don't let insecurities keep you paralyzed so that you never move beyond your comfort zone. Trust and obey God, and He will allow you to use your gifts and even increase them in His service. He will give you courage and resolution. God's love will always win over the fear of a human being.

Impatience

A lack of patience may cause you to quit if you don't see immediate results. Believing you will have instant success is contrary to the scriptural principle of sowing and reaping. It is long, hard work for spiritual parents to nurture and train spiritual babies, and it may be many months or even years before those children grow up to care for themselves and eventually become spiritual parents. It will take time for your vision for your children to be fulfilled, so you need to remember that there are three stages to the fulfillment of any vision, including the vision to become an effective spiritual parent: (1) the honeymoon stage; (2) the trial (testing) stage (in which we feel like quitting); and (3) the fruitfulness stage.

The Bible is filled with examples of those who started out high on the excitement of the vision, refused to quit during the trial stage, and then experienced great fruitfulness. The story of Joseph is one of the best of these examples. After having an exciting, inspiring dream in which his brothers bowed down to him, Joseph encountered trial after trial. He was sold as a slave by his brothers, lied about by his employer's wife, imprisoned while innocent and forgotten in prison—yet he eventually became second-in-command of all of Egypt! He enjoyed the stage of great fruitfulness because he refused to give up during the testing season of his life. God used this stage of trial in Joseph's life to build him into the man of integrity the Lord had called him to be, the man who could bear the fruit planned for him. Only after all of the trials could Joseph be a blessing to the brothers who had treated him so unjustly years before.

Joseph passed the test, and so can you! Don't quit during the testing stage and fail to experience the stage of fruitfulness the Lord has planned for you. Remember: The *process* makes us into the people who can accomplish the vision.

The Lord is much more concerned about what He is doing *in you* than He is concerned about you reaching your goals for your spiritual parenting relationship. Oswald Chambers once said, "If I can stay calm, faithful, and unconfused while in the middle of the turmoil of life, the goal of the purpose of God is being accomplished in me. God is not working toward a particular finish—His purpose is the process itself."[1] The Lord is calling you to complete dependence on Him as you persevere in your parenting relationships.

Fear

Fear, especially a fear of making mistakes, may hinder you from answering the call to become a spiritual parent. But you can trust that your efforts will be blessed if you take the risk, even if you trip up in the process. Bible teacher Bob Mumford once said, "I do not trust anyone unless he walks with a limp." Jacob, after wrestling with the Lord and demanding His blessing, was touched in his thigh and received the Lord's blessing. But from that day on, he walked with a limp (see Gen. 32:25-31).

Peter, Jesus' disciple who became an apostle of the New Testament Church after denying Jesus and experiencing His complete acceptance and forgiveness, lost his abrasiveness and became a true father in the faith. He "walked with a limp." When God lovingly deals with you through difficult times—that you may or may not have caused—you will walk with a spiritual limp for the rest of your life. Experiences in spiritual parenting often result in walking with a limp. You will make your share of mistakes while parenting, but you must not be deterred or become weary.

Sometimes you may find yourself doing all the right things, but problems still arise. If so, you may be tempted to go back to something easier than dealing with the shortcomings of humanity. Spiritual mothering and fathering is not easy, but it *is* rewarding. Even Jesus dealt with problems while fathering the Twelve. They all left Him in the Garden of Gethsemane. He felt alone and forsaken, but He knew the last chapter was not yet written: Fifty days later, Peter stood with the other 11 apostles to preach during Pentecost, and 3,000 people came to faith in Christ!

Fear of being hurt, especially if you've been hurt before, may hinder you from developing into a spiritual mother or father: "I've tried to be a spiritual dad to someone and I was hurt. I don't want to be hurt again." Well, I have news for you: You will probably get hurt again! If you are a natural parent, you know that sometimes you experience pain and disappointment as you raise your kids. It comes with the territory. With spiritual kids, the territory will feel awfully familiar. Your spiritual children will not always like what you have to say. They may become tiresome and forget appointments. They may sometimes act as if they don't care. Those things are all part of the parenting experience.

Jesus was abandoned by His followers after He was arrested in the Garden of Gethsemane. But Christ forgave them. God Himself was abandoned by one-third of his "staff" when

Lucifer rebelled and was thrown out of heaven (see Rev. 12:3-4). The apostle Paul, who was a spiritual father to many, tells us that his spiritual children abandoned him when he was in a real pinch. He had to appear before the emperor, and the Christians at Rome were afraid, so they deserted him: "At my first defense, no one came to my support, but everyone deserted me. May it not be held against them" (2 Tim. 4:16). Paul could have been deeply hurt by the abandonment of his followers, but he chose to not count it against them.

Natural and spiritual children have the potential to give you the greatest joy and the greatest pain. The inconsistent or irritating behavior in your spiritual children may come from a deep struggle to overcome stubborn sins. Don't throw in the towel just yet. Look beyond the superficial symptoms and be willing to challenge your spiritual children to face their problems—and then lay them at the foot of the cross. After all, their problems are God's problem. Trust God to raise *His* child *His* way.

You may have some discouraging and frustrating times as a spiritual parent, but through them you will learn to lean wholly on the Lord. Trust Him to take the pain of yesterday and any pain that lies ahead and shape it for His glory.

Embracing Your Call to Spiritual Parenthood

A man of God once said, "To do anything less than what you were created to do will bore you." Many in the Body of Christ are bored because they are not fulfilling what God created them to be: spiritual parents! Spiritual fathers and mothers rarely get bored; instead, they have a sense of fulfillment and dignity. Spiritual parents around the world are finding this out!

Ibrahim Omondi, a journalist from Nairobi, Kenya, knew his people were not living up to their potential. Having a keen interest in spiritual parenting and the cell-church concept, he sought a working model and asked to observe me as I served our new church, built on the principles of spiritual parenting and small-group ministry.

Our church had been birthed a few years earlier with three new cell groups. But we had had setbacks. Instead of multiplying, one cell group had died. We desperately pleaded for God's help as we reminded our people, "You are ministers, and God desires to use you!" Eventually, faith rose in their hearts, they obeyed God's calling, and the Lord began to move. People gave their lives to Christ. New believers came to the cells. New leaders were trained. At last—multiplication!

Two cells became four. Four became eight. Eight became sixteen and sixteen became thirty-two. The church grew rapidly. As pastor, I spent most of my time meeting with cell leaders to discuss the needs and potential of individual cell members. Each leader and I regularly prayed simple faith-filled prayers for each believer in that leader's cell group. Spiritual parents cared for these believers just as natural parents care for their children.

Ibrahim sat, watching and listening, and finally my African brother opened his heart. Weeping, he unburdened himself:

> Western evangelists come to my nation and hold massive crusades. The TV cameras roll. When the evangelist asks my brothers to raise their hands to receive Christ, many respond. The next week, another evangelist comes to town, and many of those same brothers come to the crusade and raise their hands again. My people need a sense of dignity, where every individual believer understands he is important to God and to His purposes. Will you come and help us? We need a new model of church life.

Ibrahim and his wife, Diane, opened their home for cell ministry. Neighbors and friends received the Lord, and many found a spiritual family. Cells birthed in neighboring areas of the city multiplied throughout Kenya and then throughout Uganda and Rwanda. Today, Ibrahim trains leaders to start cell groups and new churches all over East Africa, and he and Diane serve as spiritual parents to pastors and spiritual leaders throughout Africa. God is using the Omondis internationally today because they began locally as spiritual parents.

Even more rapid than the spiritual awakening in East Africa, the revival in China today is considered the largest spiritual harvest since the earliest such harvest recorded in the book of Acts. The Cultural Revolution, with its severe persecution of Christians, fueled the revival through the various house-church movements that have sprung up throughout the nation. Some estimate that there are over 100 million believers in China.[2]

According to an article posted by *Christianity Today*:

The dazzling growth of Christianity inside China began in the late 1970s at the end of the Cultural Revolution. During that period, up to 7 million people died from widespread violence and famine.

At that time, there were an estimated 3 million Catholics and Protestants in China. Three decades later, estimates of the number of Christians vary widely, anywhere from 54 million to 130 million, the higher number representing a 43-fold increase, which would be one of the largest growth spurts in the history of Christianity.

Scholars have debated for decades about the number of Christians in China. But the new estimates both come from government sources. The higher number of 130 million reportedly comes from Ye Xiaowen, the head of China's State Administration of Religious Affairs. According to reliable reports, he used the 130 million head count at two government briefings in 2006. Bob Fu of China Aid Association has cited 130 million as a credible estimate. Other experts believe any statistic reporting over 100 million Christians is not credible.[3]

In January 2001, I had the opportunity to minister to 80 key leaders of the underground church movement in China. It was life-changing for me. Meeting these humble men and women of God deeply moved me. I know one thing for sure: They taught me far more than I could teach them.

Ninety-five percent of these leaders, many of whom had traveled four days by train to get to the secluded leadership training

seminar, had been imprisoned for their faith. One elderly leader had been released just four days before the seminar's start.
One precious man of God who sat at our breakfast table told us
humbly that he mentors the leaders of 10 million believers in the
house-church network he oversees. I sat in amazement! It was as
if I was in another world.

I also met with a small group of women at the seminar who
oversee house-church leaders, one of whom was responsible for
4,000 believers in her network. They told stories of being bru-
tally raped in prison, yet they had stayed true to the Lord and
continue to birth house churches as new people come to Christ
all over their nation.

I was asked by these Chinese Christian leaders to teach on
the biblical mandate to be spiritual mothers and fathers. After
the sessions, these humble women and men of God stood, prayed
and repented. It was such a humbling and life-changing experience. They repented because they had gotten caught up in the
work of God and were no longer focused enough on the workers
of God. This is a great lesson for all of us to learn: Let us never
get so caught up in God's work that we lose sight of our call to
spiritually parent the next generation.

A few years ago, I was asked to share the vision of the New
Testament Church in Auckland, New Zealand. While there, I met
Robert, who listened intently as I spoke about Jesus spending
most of His time with His disciples, His spiritual sons. I discussed God's call on every believer to be a minister as stated in
Ephesians 4:11-12. I also looked at Acts 2, which reflects the New
Testament model of church, and emphasized that small-group
ministry and spiritual families should be part of the paradigm
for today's church. After about 30 minutes, Robert spoke, filled
with emotion:

When I was 13 years old, the Lord called me to be a minister. For more than 20 years, I tried to find doors that
would open for me to fulfill this call. As I understood
it, the only way to be a minister was to be ordained after completing years of theological training. Sometime

back, I led a man to the Lord. I discipled him and watched him grow. It was so fulfilling. I realize tonight, I no longer need to try to be a minister—I am one!

I could tell that a heavy load had dropped from Robert's back. The truth had set him free. Robert had realized he could fulfill the Lord's call to minister by discipling a new believer. He had become a spiritual father.

Depend on the Father

I hope these testimonies about the vitality and necessity of spiritual parenting, gathered from around the world, have helped to kindle a fire in your heart. It is my fervent prayer that you—and every other believer in Christ—will be captured by the revelation of the Father's call to minister! And the Father will always be there to help spiritual parents and children serve each other and encourage each other toward maturity.

Ron Myer, a faithful friend and colleague who has served with me in leadership for nearly 30 years, believes that the story of the prodigal son is told the way it is because of the big difference between being a father and being an older brother—especially the kind of brother exemplified in the prodigal son story:

> In many cases, a brother will inspire you, but a father will direct you. A brother may wound you, but a father will heal you. A brother often sees you for who you are, a father sees your potential. A brother has a tendency to judge you, while a father will lovingly correct you. A brother may condemn you for wasting your inheritance on riotous living, but a father will love you, woo you back home, and restore you.
>
> Aren't you glad the prodigal son ran into his father before his older brother? Had he run into his older brother first, the outcome of the story could have ended much differently.[4]

The Lord is taking older brothers and sisters in our generation and raising them up to become spiritual fathers and mothers.

But it is not always easy to be a spiritual parent. It requires sacrifice and something that is often in short supply: time. Nevertheless, when you look to the larger purposes God has for your life, you will see many benefits of your obedience.

Jesus understood that His disciples had left their families to follow Him, and He reminded them about the benefits of their obedience:

> Assuredly, I say to you, there is not one who has left house or brothers or sisters or father or mother or wife or children or lands, for My sake and the gospel's, who shall not receive a hundredfold now in this time—houses and brothers and sisters and mothers and children and lands, with persecutions—and in the age to come, eternal life (Mark 10:29-30, *NKJV*).

The person who gives up her or his comfort zone will gain spiritual children! Jesus assured His disciples that they would produce spiritual children, an eternal inheritance that could be passed down as their legacy. This was their reward.

God wants to produce exceptional spiritual fathers and mothers, but that requires obedience and sacrifice. Numbers 26:63-65 describes how out of the first generation of Israelites in the wilderness, only Joshua and Caleb were left to enter the Promised Land—they were the only ones who had been obedient and had followed the Lord wholeheartedly. Why hadn't the rest of their generation made it to the Promised Land? Because they had believed a bad report: When the spies had returned to Moses and the Israelites and showed them the fruit of the Promised Land, 10 of the spies had given a discouraging report about giants in the land and had said the Israelites wouldn't be able to conquer them.

Don't believe a bad report. The enemy will try to get you to believe his lies—*How could you ever be a spiritual parent? You're too busy. You're not spiritual enough; You've made too many mistakes*—but God has called you to the Promised Land. Depend on your heavenly Father. He loves to use weak people who find their strength in Him. You may never feel entirely ready to be a spiritual parent—you just need to be willing. Ask the Lord to lead you and to fill your heart with the purpose of becoming the spiritual parent to someone in the next generation of leaders.

Depend on the Bridegroom

The Lord is committed to His Church. He has promised to return for the Bride (His Church), who is "without stain or wrinkle" (Eph. 5:27). On the day I was married, I looked for my bride at the back of the auditorium, ready to walk up the aisle to become my wife. If she had slipped in the mud a few minutes before her entry, what do you think my reaction would have been? To reject her? Certainly not! I would have done whatever it took to clean her up to prepare her for the wedding!

Our Lord, the Bridegroom, is preparing the Bride. She has been soiled and badly wrinkled during the past 2,000 years, but He is committed to cleaning her up! She will be a glorious Church when she is presented to Him, perfect in every way!

As part of the purifying process, the Lord is raising up a new generation of spiritual parents among us. They are marked by *humility* and *servanthood*. They embrace and honor their own spiritual parents who believe in them and coach them. They have no desire to build their own empires. These new leaders see their gifts as just a few of the many critical pieces needed as the family searches after the mind of Christ together. They honor and lift up other ministries, churches, leaders and believers in their regions. They are secure in their identities and in the Lord's call on their lives as they bless those around them.

Imagine with me for a moment the church in your community in the coming days as she returns to the biblical truth of spiritual parenting. Churches in your community will recognize that there is no competition in the kingdom of God—only completion—and all believers, individually and corporately, will fulfill the call of God on their lives. Every gift the Lord has given to the members of the Body of Christ will be properly used for the glory of God. New believers will be birthed into the family of God and nurtured into spiritual parenthood day after day. True family will be restored to the Body of Christ.

This is the picture that will become a reality as the Bride is prepared for her ultimate reunion with her Bridegroom! You can trust and depend on Him to mold and purify you as that time draws near.

Searching for a Spiritual Child

I like the way Mark Hanby, international teacher and speaker on church government, describes a spiritual father:

> A spiritual father is someone whose life and ministry raised you up from the mire of immaturity into proper growth and order. A spiritual father is the one whose words pierced beyond the veneer of a blessing into the very heart and marrow of your existence, causing a massive realignment to your spirit. A spiritual father is not necessarily the one who birthed you into the kingdom. Instead, he is the one who rescues you from the doorstop of your abandonment and receives you into his house, gives you a name, and makes you his son.[5]

God wants to give us a legacy of spiritual children, but we must find them and make them our children.

At one point, the prophet Elijah was very discouraged and depressed, and he feared for his life (see 1 Kings 19). He had just experienced the spiritual high of the miracle on Mount Carmel, but he fled into the desert when he was threatened by evil Queen Jezebel. There under a juniper tree, he complained to God of his ill fortune and how he felt as if he was the only godly man left in the land.

What solution did God give him? "Go, find a son" (see 1 Kings 19:15-16). God believed in Elijah, even when he was in the midst of a deep depression. Like the good Father He is, God refused to allow Elijah's spiritual legacy to die so easily. Instead, the Lord encouraged him to train a son (Elisha) to be his successor. Elijah obeyed, placed his coat on Elisha and anointed him as his assistant (see 1 Kings 19:16,19). Once again, he had purpose and direction. His anointing would be multiplied through a son.

I find it interesting that when the Lord took Elijah away in the whirlwind, Elisha cried out, "My father! My father!" not "My prophet! My prophet!" (2 Kings 2:12). Elijah had truly become a father to the younger man.

As Elijah fathered his spiritual son into maturity, Elisha asked his spiritual parent for a double portion of the spirit that was on him, and Elijah imparted it to him. Elisha experienced twice the number of miracles that his spiritual father had seen. Likewise, you should expect your spiritual children to progress far beyond you spiritually.

Someday you and I will stand before the living God. When I stand before the Lord, I do not want to stand there by myself—I want to stand surrounded by a multitude of my spiritual children, grandchildren and even more future descendants! How about you? Like Elijah, it's time for you to find a spiritual daughter or son!

In his book *The Spiritual Mentor*, Ron DePriest says:

> God is breathing the heart of spiritual duplication into the earth. . . .
>
> A true father's heart will not rule you, but will serve you and your vision. He will labor to help you fulfill your destiny, not his own destiny. True fathers are concerned about the inheritance being transferred to the next generation. They are concerned about preparing that generation to receive all that the Father has for them.[6]

God has divine plans for our lives. I was a chicken farmer when the Lord called LaVerne and me to serve as spiritual parents. Our God is no respecter of persons. Some spiritual parents are housewives, others are high-school students, others run corporations, and still others work in law firms, factories and department stores. The call was the same for them as it is for you. God is calling you to get involved and invested in others' lives as a spiritual father or mother. It is the key to your spiritual inheritance.

Key Questions for Practical Application

1. What are some things that hinder you from becoming a spiritual parent, and what can you do about the obstacles?
2. How can a spiritual child give you great pain and great joy?
3. Is it possible to become so caught up in the work of the Lord that you lose sight of your calling to be a spiritual parent?

A FINAL CHALLENGE

I challenge you to join a revolution that will change the world.

Jesus started a revolution 2,000 years ago by discipling 12 men. Paul followed Jesus' example when he discipled Timothy, Titus and Silas. Since then, this concept of spiritual parenting has been sporadically picked up by faithful believers in Christ. Today, unfortunately, Jesus' style of disciple making has been all but lost in the Body of Christ and has largely been replaced with a focus on meetings and programs. Now is the time for each member of Christ's Church to pick up the responsibility of spiritual parenting, make disciples and continue the revolution started by Jesus Christ.

Jesus set the revolution in motion by modeling what He expected: Jesus spent most of His time with His 12 young disciples—His spiritual sons. Although Jesus chose John, believed to be only 17 years of age, to be His closest disciple, Peter and James were also part of Jesus' inner circle. Through this simple concept, Jesus reproduced Himself in His followers to start a revolution that changed the world. Call it what you want—mentoring, discipling, coaching, or spiritual fathering or mothering—it all basically boils down to the same thing: caring about the spiritual growth of another person.

Paul grasped this truth of disciple making when he told Timothy:

> You then, my son, be strong in the grace that is in Christ Jesus. And the things you have heard me say in the presence of many witnesses entrust to reliable men who will also be qualified to teach others (2 Tim. 2:1-2).

Paul exhorted Timothy, who was his spiritual son, to find other disciples who would disciple others.

Every one of us is called to become a spiritual mother or father and to make disciples (see Matt. 28:19-20). I challenge you to ask God for just one reproducing disciple (a person willing to parent someone else down the road), according to the pattern of Jesus and Paul. Just one! Sure, if you want to disciple more, go for it. But start with one. It might be a coworker, a family member, someone from church or a friend. Pray to God and ask for His help and He will show you where to start. Ask the potential spiritual daughter or son to meet with you every few weeks (maybe for coffee or tea) and talk about your walk with Jesus. Pray daily for your disciple. And encourage your spiritual daughter or son to disciple someone else next year.

Every year, you can repeat the pattern as you find another person to disciple who will also become a reproducing disciple. By discipling only one person each year who is also discipling one person, in 10 years you will have discipled directly or indirectly more than 1,000 people! After 20 years of parenting only one disciple each year, you will be responsible for more than one million disciples! Do the math if you do not believe me. After 30 years, the number jumps to more than one billion! No wonder the enemy has been hiding this truth from God's people and keeping us busy in activity—even religious activity.

Now for the naysayers who are saying, "But we do not live in a perfect world. If some disciples drop out, won't the exponential growth chain be broken?" My response remains positive: I will take a half million disciples if the chain breaks down.

I have been blessed to be making disciples for more than 40 years. It is not always easy. Like natural children, spiritual children have the potential to give great joy and great pain to their parents. But the pain is worth it.

This is my one-person challenge for you: Ask God to help you find your Timothy. Join Jesus' exponential discipleship revolution! God has called you, so what are you waiting for?

EPILOGUE

The Progression of Impartation

In his book *You Have Not Many Fathers*, minister and speaker Dr. Mark Hanby explains what happens all too frequently when the Church refuses to recognize that the flow of power in the kingdom of God is through relationship:

> Without the spiritual relationship of father to son, there can never be the passing of double portions or a true basis of spiritual authority and identity. . . . The flow of all power in the kingdom of God is through relationship with one another. The amputation of relationship has left the church handicapped in power. The disjointed connection in the order of God's people has made some members lame and withered in spiritual atrophy. Other members have become exhausted, overburdened with an unbalanced share of kingdom responsibility and care. To manifest a complete Christ to the whole world, spiritual connections must be restored and the balance of power shared by each member.[1]

I agree wholeheartedly! I believe the balance of power can be shared as spiritual impartations are passed on from fathers and mothers to sons and daughters.

A Working Example of Impartation

The easiest way to explain how a spiritual impartation is passed on is to give you a working example from the cell-based church I pastored in Lancaster County, Pennsylvania.

The Journey of One Cell Group

I served as the pastor of DOVE Christian Fellowship, a cell-based church in our community in south-central Pennsylvania, for many years. By "cell-based," I mean that everyone committed to the church is committed to other believers in a small cell group. We used the term "cell group" because cells in our body grow and eventually go through the process of mitosis, in which one cell becomes two, two become four and so on, as the process of multiplication continues. This process of cell multiplication is modeled for us in the book of Acts, where we read about the New Testament Church meeting in homes in every city (see Acts 20:20).

Our journey started in the late 1970s, when LaVerne and I found ourselves the spiritual parents of a group of young Christians, and we started a cell group in our home. By 1980, we had multiplied into two cell groups in two different homes. Soon there were three cell groups, and we started a new church that held a Sunday morning celebration with about 25 people in attendance. By the grace of God, these cell groups continued to grow as people throughout our community came to Christ and joined a spiritual family (cell) and our new church. Ten years later, in 1990, there were 125 cell groups making up more than 2,300 people committed to our church. Churches were planted in Scotland, Brazil and Kenya. (If you want to read more about our story, you can read *House to House,* which tells about our church's adventure in cell groups.[2])

The Journey of One Spiritual Father

Through the process of our church growing and multiplying, hundreds of spiritual fathers and mothers were released as ministers to God's people through cell groups. Carl Good, one of these spiritual fathers, began his parenting journey as a cell-group member.

Carl was in his early 50s when he and his wife, Doris, who were from the small town of Manheim, Pennsylvania, started attending our church and participating in the cell ministry. Carl worked at a feed manufacturing plant and Doris was a buying agent for a local business. Although they were unassuming, quiet members of their cell group, they were committed to growing strong relationships.

After a time, their commitment to relationships and their willingness to serve caught the attention of Carl and Doris's cell leaders. They were asked to consider leading a cell. With fear and trembling, they agreed to this new venture and completed our church's cell-leader training course. After a few months as assistant cell leaders, Carl and Doris assumed the leadership responsibilities for their cell. They were a do-what-you-can-with-what-you-have-where-you-are kind of couple; and while they weren't flashy, they loved people, and their living room soon filled to capacity. People were naturally drawn to them, because they were authentic and caring. In time, they parented assistant leaders in the group, raising up enough leaders to start another cell. Before long, they had launched two more cells, then a third and a fourth. Over the next few years, their cells continually grew and multiplied.

Meanwhile, our church family was rapidly expanding, and we needed to add to our staff more support pastors who could spiritually father the cell leaders. (At DOVE, the cell-group leaders are parented by the church leadership—everyone has a spiritual parent!) As we prayed and looked for spiritual parents among the cells, our eyes fell on Carl, a true pastor. He was *already* fathering the cell leaders, having been trained in the seminary and boot camp of the cell group. Carl joined our paid staff and continued to be a father to the cell leaders in the greater Manheim area.

A few years later, the Lord called our church family to decentralize and plant eight autonomous new cell churches in our region, all at the same time. Who became the senior pastor of the new church in Manheim? You guessed it—Carl. Under Carl's leadership, this new Manheim cell church soon began a new cell-based church—in the nation of Scotland! A Scottish couple who had attended our Church Planting and Leadership School had joined a cell group in the Manheim church, which Carl was pastoring. The couple had then returned to Scotland to plant a new cell, which grew and multiplied, eventually evolving into a new church. The leaders of the Scottish church looked across the ocean to Carl as a spiritual father. The church in Manheim continued to start cells all over the community, and it actually planted two new churches in Pennsylvania.

A few years ago, Carl turned the leadership of the Manheim church over to one of the elders whom he had fathered, and Carl began to serve as a father to church leaders. Various church leaders throughout our nation and the world already looked to Carl as their spiritual father, and he knew it was time to focus on these parenting relationships. He served with us on the DOVE Christian Fellowship International Apostolic Council, which gives oversight to church leaders of cell-based churches and church movements scattered across five continents.

A few years ago, Carl went to be with Jesus. As I stood before his family and friends at his memorial service, I read letters and emails from people all over the world who said the same thing over and over again: "I had been looking for a spiritual father all of my Christian life, and God answered my prayers. Carl was a spiritual father to me."

When the Lord had called him to learn how to be a spiritual father, Carl was an ordinary man, a worker in a feed manufacturing plant and a member of a cell group. He was obedient to the Lord's call, though, and became a grassroots spiritual father who fathered new believers in Christ through cell groups meeting from house to house (see Rom. 16:3-11). Later, after multiplying his cell group several times, he became a pastor who focused on fathering cell-group leaders across the city, thus becoming a kind of spiritual grandfather (see Titus 1:5). Still later, Carl parented the pastors of churches just as Paul, Barnabas, Titus and Timothy had in the Early Church. Carl had actually become a spiritual great-grandfather! When he went home to be with the Lord years later, he had in fact become an *international* apostolic leader!

I should clarify that Carl's story is unique to Carl. Not everyone trained in the small group will become an apostolic father, a local pastor or even a small-group leader. Some small-group leaders will remain small-group leaders and impart their legacy within their group by training more small-group leaders, because this is their call from God. They still become spiritual fathers and grandfathers because, eventually, those whom they father in the Lord will become spiritual parents to another generation. The lineage goes on and on. Perhaps some of these small-group leaders will develop into a pastor of a local church or an apostolic leader, but not all will. My point is that every believer is called to some kind of spiritual parenting, so you simply need to follow God's call on your life and not be pushed into a role of leadership that does not fit you! David tried on Saul's armor, but it did not fit. You cannot wear someone else's "armor."

Carl had not aspired to pastor a church, much less to pastor other pastors. He just had loved Jesus and wanted to be obedient. But God had plans for him—divine plans for spiritual impartation that took Carl from cell-group member to apostolic father.

Grassroots Spiritual Parents

The New Testament Church was a grassroots movement that met from house to house. Ordinary people led others to Christ and lovingly parented the new believers in Paul-Timothy-type relationships by opening up their homes and generously serving each other. They shared their friendship with Jesus, extending His grace and forgiveness to the world. In these small-group settings, they built loving relationships with one another and learned from the ground up how to become spiritual parents. I like to refer to parents trained in this setting as grassroots spiritual parents.

When our church started, we were a fledgling cell-based movement that grew by developing grassroots spiritual mothers and fathers. In the late 1970s, the Lord spoke to me, asking if I would be willing to "be involved in the underground church." At the time, I knew little about cell groups and how the family-type relationships built within them could impact lives. But I began to picture an underground church as the unseen half of a tree, the underground root system that nourishes the whole tree and keeps it healthy. Like the roots of a tree, the underground church is composed of believers gathered together in small groups to pray, evangelize and build healthy relationships with each other. These mutually accountable mother-daughter and father-son relationships are vital in order for each member to experience spiritual growth, encouragement and reproduction, and vital for the health of the whole tree: the church.

We taught the believers in our church that each individual could develop into a spiritual mother or father at the grassroots level, and we encouraged each church member to actually become a spiritual parent. As more and more of the believers within the cell groups began to rise to God's call for spiritual mothers and fathers, the groups multiplied. No one was left on her or his own to figure out how spiritual parenting worked—the network of roots that began with a few teenagers hanging out at our house meant that everyone was connected, from the underground up!

Likewise, you will not be hung out to dry when you take the step of obedience and become a spiritual mother or father. The Lord will help you sink a network of relationships deep into the ground to nourish and strengthen you for ministry.

Local Church Spiritual Parents

Our church grew rapidly as grassroots parents reproduced themselves over and over again. Soon we needed another kind of spiritual parent to accommodate the swell. We began to develop the next level of spiritual parents: pastors and elders. Carl moved into this aspect of spiritual fatherhood when God entrusted him with the responsibility to oversee, not only one or two spiritual families (cells) at a time, but also a whole team of spiritual parents (cell-group leaders). He became the pastor-father of a congregation that was made of many cells.

This new branch of spiritual fathering and mothering released us to become eight congregations in Pennsylvania and three in other nations. (These groups were to become the base for DOVE International, the international church movement that I now oversee with a team of apostolic leaders from around the world.) We viewed the leadership of these eleven congregations as local church fathers, and they in turn regarded their churches, not as places or meeting times, but as families of believers. The local church leaders were spiritual parents who were called to oversee the many spiritual families (cell groups) and cell leaders within their church.

A local church pastor has the heart of a shepherd to care for the cell leaders, who in turn care for the pastor's sheep, the congregation. When I served as a senior pastor, I often told our team of pastors, "You should not be in your office all day. You should be out spiritually parenting small-group leaders." We encouraged pastors to meet with small-group leaders on their turf. On various occasions when I served as a pastor, I had three breakfasts in one morning as I met individually with three cell leaders in a restaurant close to where they all lived. One time, I hopped on a cell leader's tractor and spent time with him as he plowed his field! Spending time parenting small-group leaders in the church raises healthy spiritual families.

Some of these local spiritual parents became church planters and began a whole new branch of the family so that the needs of the new generation coming into the kingdom of God would be met.

Apostolic Spiritual Parents

By the time our church was 15 years old, we had grown to a point where we knew we needed another branch of spiritual parenting to accomplish what God had called us to do. The vision the Lord had given us—"to build a relationship with Jesus, with one another, and transform our world from house to house, city to city, and nation to nation"—could not be fulfilled under our current church structure. So we gave our church away!

We had always taught about empowering and releasing individual believers to reach their full potential. Now we gave that freedom to pastoral leaders in our church who had become spiritual parents in our church and who could spiritually parent their own local church in rural Pennsylvania. We were convinced that the Lord was asking us to decentralize our mega-church and release eight leaders to become spiritual parents of eight different cell-based local churches in our area and give each the option to join the DOVE Christian Fellowship International family of churches and ministries or to connect to another part of the Body of Christ. As natural parents train and release their daughter to a husband in marriage, we gave the church away to a new generation of leaders who had become spiritual fathers and mothers themselves. The eight new local churches and most of the overseas church plants expressed a desire to stay together and partner with the DOVE International family of churches worldwide.

Our transition as a church required us to form an apostolic council to give spiritual oversight to the leadership of all of the self-governing congregations. This team birthed a new category of spiritual parenting in the church: apostolic servant-leaders. The spiritual parents who serve on our Apostolic Council give spiritual oversight and protection, and they serve as an outside court of appeal for the senior leaders and leadership teams of our local churches.

C. Peter Wagner, in his book *The New Apostolic Churches,* calls this apostolic movement the New Apostolic Reformation. He says that this new work of God is "changing the shape of Protestant Christianity around the world."[3] And it's something that is forward looking: "Traditional Christianity starts with the present situation and focuses on the past. New apostolic Christianity starts with the present situation and focuses on the future."[4] New apostolic leaders are dedicated to releasing their congregations to do the ministry of the church.

More than 20 apostolic fathers are mentioned in the New Testament: Paul, Barnabas, Silas, James, Timothy, and many others had responsibility before the Lord to serve the local leaders of the Early Church. Paul's letters are an example of New Testament apostolic spiritual fathering.

Like healthy, natural parents who relate to their married children, apostolic parents influence rather than control. These seasoned apostolic spiritual parents coach pastors and spouses of local churches, and they do so by developing supportive relationships with local church elders. These are God-ordained relationships, not built through traditional denominational structures.

Many pastors have had a hard time spiritually parenting future leaders in their churches, because they themselves have never been parented. The only models of leadership they have seen are hands-on management and control from the top. Because there are many lonely leaders today—pastors and pastors' spouses of both independent and denominational churches—who are looking for apostolic spiritual parents, some denominations are wisely changing their structures to provide for pastors' spiritual parenting built on God-ordained relationships. The Lord has heard the leaders' cries and is raising up apostolic spiritual parents who have a call and passion to serve these parentless ministers. These local pastors need more mature ministers to sit with them regularly, to listen to them, to cry with them, to coach them and to hold them accountable to walk in integrity.

Apostolic parents encourage leaders to press into the Lord and to trust His Word, and they have hearts to bring into completion—not compete with—the ministry the Lord is building in a local church. They are equippers and encouragers who come alongside the pastor to see the pastor's vision fulfilled. As representatives of Jesus Christ, apostolic spiritual fathers and mothers come with hearts of servants and a desire to see their spiritual children far exceed them in ministry.

I am especially burdened for this kind of spiritual parenting, because during the majority of the years I was senior pastor of a megachurch, I did not have anyone to father me. I paid dearly for this lack. The Lord, however, is always redemptive. He has used what I lacked then to motivate me now to train apostolic fathers who will help to parent the next generation of church leaders. Today, I am privileged to oversee the leadership team that parents the leaders of seven regional apostolic teams worldwide, who in turn oversee more than a dozen other apostolic teams throughout the nations who are serving hundreds of church leaders on six continents.

Psalm 68:6 tells us that the Lord is placing "the lonely in families." The Lord is restoring spiritual parenting to His Church to meet the needs of lonely new believers, lonely church members, lonely small-group leaders and lonely pastors. A few years ago, I was in Bulgaria and a pastor told me as we drove to the airport, "The loneliness I have had in my heart for years is gone. The Lord has provided spiritual fathers for me."

Each congregation, denomination, movement and "stream" within the Body of Christ is very important to the Lord. We are all needed and should strive to work together, because we are all members of the family of God! Regardless of the terminology you use for Christian leaders in your denomination or movement, pastors and leaders throughout the Body of Christ are crying out for apostolic spiritual fathers and mothers, and God is answering their cries by raising up those willing to answer His call.

Regional Spiritual Parents

The Lord is doing an awesome thing in our day: He is restoring the unity He prayed for: "That they all may be one, as You, Father, are in Me, and I in You; that they also may be one in Us, that the world may believe that You sent Me" (John 17:21, *NKJV*). Walls that for centuries have divided denominations and church groups are coming down throughout the world at an incredible rate. Pastors in the same town who never knew one another are now finding each other, praying together regularly and supporting one another's ministries. This kind of unity is exciting!

Just this morning, while ministering at a church in the Pacific Northwest, I was asked to join an early morning prayer meeting in their city. More than 100 believers from more than 10 different churches have been gathering together to pray for revival every day from five to six o'clock in the morning. The spiritual atmosphere is sweet as these precious believers meet to pray together.

During the next several years, I believe that there will be an emergence of spiritual leaders from various backgrounds and denominations who will form teams to serve various cities and regions of the world. There will be apostolic spiritual fathers and mothers who serve towns, cities and regions. They will no longer think only in terms of pastoring their own churches but will think and pray in terms of pastoring their region with fellow servant-leaders throughout the Body of Christ. Although these "spiritual parents of the region" will be concerned about unity, unity will not be their main focus. Their main focus will be on the Lord and on His mandate to sow and reap as He brings in His harvest.

When an automobile manufacturing plant runs a car through one of its assembly lines, the car is put together with parts that have been gathered from companies all over the world. These parts are assembled in one city to make a car. In a similar way, God has brought denominations and church families from all over the world to your town or city to assemble His church in your region. Each church and ministry should be honored as an important part of the whole.

As believers walk together in unity in their regions, the Lord will command blessings. Unity among pastors and church leaders in the same region constantly surfaces as one of the most important prerequisites for revival to come to any town or city. Apostolic spiritual parents who serve the leaders of towns, cities and regions help set the stage for unity that brings revival.

Fivefold Spiritual Parents

My friend Calvin Greiner, a prophetic teacher from Manheim, Pennsylvania, after having served for a season as a senior pastor, now ministers in churches of many denominations as a trans-local fivefold minister. There are thousands of fivefold ministers in the Body of Christ today. The term "fivefold minister" refers to someone who is gifted in one or more of the five spiritual gifts listed in Ephesians 4:11-12: "And He Himself gave some to be apostles, some prophets, some evangelists, and some pastors and teachers, for the equipping of the saints for the work of ministry, for the edifying of the body of Christ" (NKJV).

The origin of the fivefold ministry gifts is Jesus Christ, who exemplified each one:

- Apostle of apostles: "As the Father has sent Me, I also send you" (John 20:21, *NKJV*). In Greek, *apostolos* refers to an ambassador of the gospel who is sent out.
- Prophet of prophets: "His disciples did not understand these things at first" (John 12:16, *NKJV*). As a prophet, Jesus explained what His followers didn't understand.
- Evangelist of evangelists: "I am the way and the truth and the life. No one comes to the Father except through me" (John 14:6).
- Teacher of teachers: "You call me Teacher and Lord, and you say well, for so I am" (John 13:13, *NKJV*).
- Pastor of pastors: "I am the good shepherd" (John 10:11).

As I travel and minister throughout the Body of Christ, I find fivefold ministers who have tapped into a spiritual parenting that is desperately missing in much of the Body of Christ: They are focusing on training potential fivefold ministers how to be apostles, prophets, evangelists, teachers or pastors to others with similar gifts and anointings. They know that if they train a few young teachers or prophets who, in turn, train others, the reproduction potential is astounding.

Fivefold spiritual parents train the next generation in their specific gifts and callings. As apostles, prophets, evangelists, pastors and/or teachers, they speak with the Lord's authority, because they represent one or more of the ministry gifts of Jesus Christ. The Lord validates them by the evidence of spiritual fruit, changed lives and signs following their ministries, such as miracles. They are recognized by local church leadership and released into ministry.

Apostolic parents train younger apostolic ministers, prophetic mothers and fathers train younger prophets in prophetic ministry, and so on so that the Body of Christ is equipped, encouraged and comes to maturity. The Lord has sent these fivefold parents (representing specific gifts) to us so that we might be complete, lacking nothing. Their goal is to train, equip and prepare the Lord's Body to be functional in everyday life as ministers of the gospel of Christ. They mentor future leadership after their own kind and help them avoid many of the pitfalls of past generations. (For a thorough understanding of the fivefold ministry from a biblical perspective, I recommend the book *Fivefold Ministry Made Practical*, written by my friend and colleague Ron Myer.[5])

God planned for us to be interconnected in relationship with one another. As spiritual mothers and fathers pass on their spiritual impartations to their children, God's kingdom advances.

ENDNOTES

Chapter 1: Calling All Believers

1. Erik Johnson, "Make Devoted Disciples: How to Be an Effective Mentor," *Christianity Today*, April 1, 2000. http://www.christianitytoday.com/biblestudies/areas/biblestudies/articles/le-2000-002-5.36.html (accessed January 2007).
2. Paul D. Stanley and J. Robert Clinton, *Connecting: The Mentoring Relationships You Need to Succeed in Life* (Colorado Springs, CO: NavPress, 1992), p. 11.
3. Ibid.

Chapter 2: Making a Spiritual Investment

1. Jimmy Stewart, "Called to Worship: The Man Behind Michael," *Charisma* Magazine, April 2000, pp. 54-55.
2. Charles Colson, "How Christianity Is Growing Around the World," The Christian Broadcasting Network. http://www.cbn.com/spirituallife/biblestudyandtheology/perspectives/colson020722.aspx (accessed December 2013).

Chapter 3: Becoming a Spiritual Family

1. Susan Hunt, *Spiritual Mothering: The Titus 2 Model for Women Mentoring Women* (Wheaton, IL: Crossway Books, 1992), p. 12.
2. Robert Stearns, *Prepare the Way: (Or Get Out of the Way!)* (Lake Mary, FL: Creation House, 1999), pp. 101-102.
3. David Cannistraci, *The Gift of Apostle: A Biblical Look at Apostleship and How God Is Using It to Bless His Church Today* (Ventura, CA: Regal Books, 1996), pp. 116-117.
4. Ken R. Canfield, "Safe in a Father's Love," *Charisma*, June 1991, pp. 68-71.
5. Cannistraci, *The Gift of Apostle*, pp. 120-124.
6. Ken Druck with James C. Simmons, *The Secrets Men Keep: Breaking the Silence Barrier* (New York: Ballantine Books, 1987).
7. *Matthew Henry's Commentary in One Volume* (Grand Rapids, MI: Zondervan, 1960), p. 119.
8. John M. Drescher, *Seven Things Children Need* (Scottdale, PA: Herald Press, 1988), p. 19.
9. Bobb Biehl, *Mentoring: Confidence in Finding a Mentor and Becoming One* (Nashville, TN: Broadman & Holman Publishers, 1996), p. 19.

Chapter 4: Growing to Spiritual Parenthood

1. Larry Kreider, *Biblical Foundation Series* (Ephrata, PA: House to House Publications, 1993). This series of 48 small-group studies covers the basics of Christian doctrine and can be used in a spiritual parenting relationship.
2. Henri J. M. Nouwen, *The Return of the Prodigal Son: A Meditation on Fathers, Brothers, and Sons* (New York: Doubleday, 1992), p. 22.

Chapter 5: Looking for a Spiritual Parent Relationship

1. See 1 Corinthians 4:17; 1 Timothy 1:2,18; 2 Timothy 1:2; 2 Timothy 2:1; Philippians 2:22.
2. See Titus 1:4; Philemon 10; Acts 20:4.
3. Mother Teresa, *In My Own Words*, comp. Jose Luis Gonzalez-Balado (New York: Random House, 1996), p. 40.
4. Gunter Krallman, *Mentoring for Mission* (Hong Kong: Jensco, Ltd., 1992), p. 50.
5. Bobb Biehl, *Mentoring: Confidence in Finding a Mentor and Becoming One* (Nashville, TN: Broadman & Holman Publishers, 1996), p. 92.

Chapter 7: Healing the Past

1. Floyd McClung, Jr., *The Father Heart of God: God Loves You—Learn to Know His Compassionate Touch* (Eugene, OR: Harvest House Publishers, 1985), pp. 129-131.
2. Ibid.
3. Larry Kreider, *House to House: Growing Healthy Small Groups and House Churches in the 21st Century* (Shippensburg, PA: Destiny Image Publishing, 2008), p. 35.
4. McClung, *The Father Heart of God*, pp. 111-114.

Chapter 8: Expanding the Number of Spiritual Parents

1. Steve and Mary Prokopchak, *Called Together* (Shippensburg, PA: Destiny Image Publishing, 2009).
2. Bobb Biehl, *Mentoring: Confidence in Finding a Mentor and Becoming One* (Nashville, TN: Broadman & Holman Publishers, 1996), p. 179.

Chapter 9: Copying the Jesus Model

1. Floyd McClung, Jr., *The Father Heart of God: God Loves You—Learn to Know His Compassionate Touch* (Eugene, OR: Harvest House Publishers, 1985), pp. 127-129.
2. John Drescher, *Seven Things Children Need* (Scottdale, PA: Herald Press, 1976), p. 19.

Chapter 10: Developing as a Spiritual Parent

1. Larry Kreider, *The Cry for Spiritual Fathers and Mothers: Compelling Vision for Authentic, Nurturing Relationships Within Today's Church* (Ephrata, PA: House to House Publications, 2000), p. 101.
2. Larry Kreider, Biblical Foundation Series (Ephrata, PA: House to House Press, 2010).
3. Sacha E. Cohen, "This Isn't Your Father's Mentoring Relationship," *AARP Magazine*, November/December 2003. http://www.aarpmagazine.org/lifestyle/Articles/a2003-09-17-mentoring.html (accessed February 2007).
4. Earl Creps, *Off-Road Disciplines: Spiritual Adventures of Missional Leaders* (San Francisco: Jossey-Bass, 2006), p. 42.
5. Ibid., p. 51.
6. For more on hearing God's voice, read Larry Kreider, *Hearing God 30 Different Ways* (Lititz, PA: House to House Publications, 2005).
7. Tom Marshall, *Understanding Leadership* (Tonbridge, Kent, England: Sovereign World Limited, 1991), p. 73.

Chapter 11: Making Decisions as a Spiritual Parent

1. Larry Kreider, Ron Myer, Steve Prokopchak and Brian Sauder, *The Biblical Role of Elders for Today's Church: New Testament Leadership Principles for Equipping Elders* (Ephrata, PA: House to House Publications, 2003).

Chapter 12: Avoiding Pitfalls

1. Steve Prokopchak, *Recognizing Emotional Dependency*, People Helping People Series (Lititz, PA: House to House Publications, 2003), p. 8.

2. Ibid.
3. Ibid.
4. Steve Prokopchak, *Counseling Basics: Helping You Help Others* (Lititz, PA: House to House Publications, 2004).

Chapter 13: Releasing Your Spiritual Children
1. Juan Carlos Ortiz, *Disciple* (Lake Mary, FL: Creation House, 1975), p. 97.
2. If you want to learn more about these new types of house-church networks springing up all over our nation, read my book *Starting a House Church: A New Model for Living Out Your Faith* (Ventura, CA: Regal Books, 2007), coauthored with Floyd McClung.

Chapter 14: Answering Your Call to Spiritual Parenthood
1. Oswald Chambers, *My Utmost for His Highest* (Grand Rapids, MI: Discovery House Publishers, 1992), July 28 reading.
2. Dick Eastman, "Three Indicators of a Coming Global Awakening!" Prayerconnect. http://www.prayerconnect.net/magazine/issue-4---water/what-god-is-doing (accessed December 2013).
3. Rob Moll, "Great Leap Forward," *Christianity Today*, May 9, 2008. www.christianitytoday.com/ct/2008/may 19 (accessed December 2013).
4. Larry Kreider, *The Cry for Spiritual Fathers and Mothers: Compelling Vision for Authentic, Nurturing Relationships Within Today's Church* (Ephrata, PA: House to House Publications, 2000), p. 163.
5. Mark Hanby with Craig Lindsay Ervin, *You Have Not Many Fathers: Recovering the Generational Blessing* (Shippensburg, PA: Destiny Image Publishers, 1996), p. 94.
6. Ron DePriest, *The Spiritual Mentor: Unlocking the Treasures of the Next Generation* (Shippensburg, PA: Destiny Image Publishers, 2005), p. 53.

Epilogue: The Progression of Impartation
1. Mark Hanby with Craig Lindsay Ervin, *You Have Not Many Fathers: Recovering the Generational Blessing* (Shippensburg, PA: Destiny Image Publishers, 1996), p. 174.
2. Larry Kreider, *House to House: Growing Healthy Small Groups and House Churches in the 21st Century* (Shippensburg, PA: Destiny Image Publishers, 2009).
3. C. Peter Wagner, *The New Apostolic Churches: Rediscovering the New Testament Model of Leadership and Why It Is God's Desire for the Church Today* (Ventura, CA: Regal Books, 1998), p. 18.
4. Ibid., p. 20.
5. Ron Myer, *Fivefold Ministry Made Practical: How to Release Apostles, Prophets, Evangelists, Pastors and Teachers to Equip Today's Church* (Lititz, PA: House to House Publications, 2006).

ABOUT THE AUTHOR

Larry Kreider is the founder and International Director of DOVE International, an international family of churches that for more than 30 years has successfully used the New Testament strategy of building the Church with small groups. DOVE, an acronym for Declaring Our Victory Emmanuel, started in the late 1970s as a youth ministry that targeted unchurched youth in south-central Pennsylvania. DOVE International grew out of the ensuing need for a flexible New Testament-style church (new wineskin) that could assist these new believers (new wine). Today, the DOVE International family consists of cell-based congregations and house churches that network throughout the United States, Central and South America, the Caribbean, Canada, Europe, Africa, Asia and the South Pacific.

Contact Information for Seminars and Speaking Engagements

Larry Kreider, International Director
DOVE International
11 Toll Gate Road
Lititz, PA 17543
Telephone: 717-627-1996
Fax: 717-627-4004

Website: www.dcfi.org

Read Larry's Blog
www.dcfi.org

Like Larry's Facebook Page
Larry and LaVerne Kreider—to receive news updates and for encouragement in spiritual parenting.